TWAYNE'S WORLD AUTHORS SERIES
A Survey of the World's Literature

FRANCE

Maxwell A. Smith, Guerry Professor of French, Emeritus
The University of Chattanooga
Former Visiting Professor in Modern Languages
The Florida State University

EDITOR

Tristan L'Hermite

TWAS 569

TRISTAN LERMITE.
Poete, et de l'Academie françoise,
Gentilhomme né à Souliers dans
la Marche il mourut l'an 1656.

Desrochers   fecit.

Herode Survecut à la vive douleur,
D'avoir donné la mort à Sa moitié cherie:
Mais Tristan, par son Energie,
Causa celle de son acteur. —

Tristan L'Hermite

TRISTAN L'HERMITE

By CLAUDE KURT ABRAHAM

University of California, Davis

TWAYNE PUBLISHERS

A DIVISION OF G. K. HALL & CO., BOSTON

Copyright © 1980 by G. K. Hall & Co.

Published in 1980 by Twayne Publishers,
A Division of G. K. Hall & Co.
All Rights Reserved

Printed on permanent/durable acid-free paper and bound in the
United States of America

First Printing

Library of Congress Cataloging in Publication Data

Abraham, Claude Kurt, 1931-
Tristan L'Hermite.

(Twayne's world authors series ; TWAS 569 : France)
Bibliography: p. 136–38
Includes index.
1. Tristan L'Hermite, François, 1601-1655—
Criticism and interpretation.
PQ1929.Z8A624   841'.4   79-22218
ISBN 0-8057-6411-9

To Amédée and Jeanne Carriat
scholars and friends
respect and love

Contents

About the Author

Born in Germany, raised in France and educated in the U.S., Claude Abraham is presently professor of French at the University of California in Davis. Though his many articles deal with all aspects of French literature, his previous books, like *Tristan L'Hermite,* focus on the seventeenth century. His *Enfin Malherbe* won the 1970 South Atlantic Modern Language Association Studies Award.

Dr. Abraham has held various offices in a dozen professional organizations and been the recipient of several post-doctoral grants.

Preface

Predecessor of Racine, anachronistic remnant of a trend dying out, precursor of Symbolism, Tristan L'Hermite has been classified and reclassified, almost always by comparison with his contemporaries. Used to shed light on others, he was seldom considered as an entity with intrinsic merits until Amédée Carriat's *Tristan ou l'Eloge d'un poète*,[1] published on the occasion of the poet's tricentenary. Even today, though numerous books and unpublished dissertations have been devoted to him, Tristan is not as popular in France as some of his contemporaries, notably Saint-Amant and Viau. As Marcel Arland suggested in his edition of Tristan's *Page disgracié*, this is undoubtedly because he is less dazzling, less shocking, and because he requires more patience and sympathy, more openmindedness for the gathering in of a careful reader's ample rewards.[2]

Whether writing for publication or for the stage, Tristan is first and foremost a poet. In an age where themes, fashions, and traditions more or less set the tone and pattern of a poem, even of its content, the poet's originality must perforce be centered on the form (musicality in general, specific rhythms, metaphors, or, more precisely, the structuring of metaphors that are themselves conventions, etc.). This poses a serious problem for a modest volume such as this, intended for the general reader, the intelligent nonspecialist whose acquaintance with literature has outdistanced his facility with French. I have tried throughout the volume to help such a reader see these elements with a minimum of jargon and obfuscation. I have translated all quotations, whether of Tristan or of secondary sources, making no attempt to preserve the poetic aura of the former or any particular style in the latter, but where I felt that such a translation would not allow the reader to grasp the point, I have given the original as well, modernizing the spelling and the punctuation (unless such a change was considered detrimental to the explication). To facilitate the bilingual reader's task, wherever the original is given, the translation is relegated to the notes. Because there exists no single edition of Tristan's complete works, and because the readers may have different anthologies and collections at their disposal, references, given in parentheses, will be to line numbers for the plays, to chapters for the prose, to collection and poem for the poetry (e.g., *Amours*, "Agréables pensées").

CLAUDE ABRAHAM

University of California, Davis

Chronology

1646 *Office de la Sainte Vierge.*
1647 *Osman* (published posthumously).
1648 *Vers héroïques.*
1649 Tristan elected to the Académie Française.
1652 *Amarillis* (published 1653).
1653 *Le Parasite* (published 1654).
1655 Death of Tristan, September 7.

CHAPTER 1

Life

THE life of Tristan L'Hermite, one of the most adventurous of his day, is a biographer's nightmare. Few documents have come down to us, most of the memoirs are notoriously unreliable—Tristan's own autobiographical novel is no exception—and contemporary correspondence, the fruit more often than not of intense polemics, can only be viewed with suspicion. Most of the dates that follow are therefore to be taken as approximations and many of the motives as ones merely surmised. The "definitive" biography of Tristan will probably never be written.[1]

I *Early Years*

The fortified castle of Soliers,[2] destroyed early in the last century, was built sometime after March, 1424, though the family can be traced beyond that. At that time, the estate seems to have been rather large, but because it repeatedly had to be divided and subdivided as numerous offspring fought for their due legacies, the L'Hermites, lords of Soliers, were neither wealthy nor powerful by the end of the sixteenth century. Pierre L'Hermite, father of the poet, was born in 1573. While still in his teens, he was inculpated in a political assassination and arrested. Condemned to death in 1595, he escaped execution only because of the intercession of Louis de Crevant and Gabrielle d'Estrées, respectively captain and mistress of both Henry III and Henry IV. Upon his release in 1597, he married Ysabeau Myron, somewhat older but of equally good birth, and "two or three years later," if we are to believe our poet, François L'Hermite was born. In later years, probably to establish an unprovable link with a famous Frenchman of the past, François took the name of Tristan L'Hermite and, more frequently yet, simply Tristan.

He was barely three years old when his grandmother took him to Paris. Not many years later—but some time before 1609[3]—he was taken into the royal household as the page of one of the King's sons, the Duc de Verneuil, who was his age. For the next few years, François shared his young master's amusements and education. One day, having wounded someone in a fit of anger, he ran away from court, sought refuge in England, and finally returned to France by way of Scotland and Norway—at least if one is to believe his own accounts in *Le Page disgracié*. Around 1617 or 1618, François entered into the employ of Nicolas de Sainte-Marthe, a poet and dramatist, who shortly thereafter introduced him to his famous uncle, Scévole de Sainte-Marthe. Reader and librarian of Scévole, the young man expanded his literary horizons and acquired a taste for poetry that he was to keep for the rest of his days. He kept this post for about two years, passing then into the service of the Marquis de Villars and from there into that of the Duc de Mayenne. In 1620, Louis XIII visited the duke, saw François, recognized his brother's former page, and took him into his own household. In 1621, thanks to Claude du Pont, one of the tutors he had shared with the royal children, François was introduced into the household of Gaston d'Orléans, brother of Louis XIII. Though the rest of his life was to be far from tranquil, it can definitely be said that the days of being the "page" were over.

II   *The Adventurous Life of a*
"Gentilhomme à la suite de Monseigneur".

Gaston d'Orléans, the young rebellious brother of Louis XIII, was a brilliant Maecenas, but his volatile temperament and the resulting political embroilments that were to plague him all of his life made his financial support unreliable and the climate of his civilized court unstable. Tristan himself was in and out of that court, frequently dropped from the rolls of pensioned gentlemen-in-waiting, but always coming back. It must be added that Gaston did not always pay the pension, and that Tristan was an incorrigible gambler. It is therefore no surprise that Tristan, buffeted by alternating waves of good and bad fortune, frequently ill, constantly vacillated between elation and despondency.[4]

Nor should it be surprising that Tristan's poetic production is a reflection of that same milieu and its way of life. One of Tristan's earliest poems, the "Ode à M. de Chaudebonne," shows him in one of his more somber moods:

Laisse faire à la Destinée
. . . .

J'irai perdre dans ma maison
Les ressentiments d'une injure
Dont je ne sais pas la raison.[5]

On the other hand, at the siege of La Rochelle where he accompanied his master, Tristan celebrated the latter's success in a masterful descriptive poem, *La Mer*, in which thoughts of gloom are forced to yield to more optimistic ones. Unfortunately for the poet, Gaston failed to benefit from his glorious enterprise. When Louis XIII and Richelieu, jealous of his victory, rushed to take command of the royal troops, and when, to prevent further gains in Gaston's popularity, they refused to give him command of various forces, the royal prince left the court. Reconciliations and ruptures alternated until 1630, when Gaston definitely broke with his brother and, followed by his court, sought refuge in Lorraine. There he wooed and eventually wed Marguerite de Vaudemont, wealthy sister of the powerful Duc de Lorraine. This act directly contradicted an express order of the king, who feared more than anything else not only the alliance, but the possibility of male progeny that might endanger his own place on the throne, since he himself was still childless. The Duc de Lorraine having signed a peace treaty with Louis, and one of the stipulations being the repudiation of Gaston, the rebellious brother sought refuge in the Spanish Lowlands. There he raised an army with the willing help of the Spaniards and soon invaded France, aided by his half-brother, Moret, and some of the most powerful nobles in France. Eventually defeated and disillusioned, he retired to his castle in Blois, concentrating on rebuilding it and on protecting the arts, letters, and sciences.

Such turmoil was obviously not suited to the composition of works of any breadth. As a result, Tristan's taste for theater remained in check except for a few obscene libretti which the poet supplied for some of Gaston's ballets. On the other hand, the exploits of Gaston were immediately celebrated in appropriate circumstantial poems. Some of these, obviously thrown together in haste, are little more than a string of banalities. A few, as we shall see later on, are among the best in the genre.

During the stay of this gallant court in the austere Spanish Lowlands, the Duc de Bouillon met Mademoiselle de Bergh and fell madly in love with her. He then asked Tristan to be his mouthpiece and, in a few months, "while springtime laughed amid the flowers"—and while Tristan obviously enjoyed some relative peace and quiet—the poet composed one of the finest lyrical collections of the century, *Les Plaintes d'Acante*, nucleus of the later—and equally successful—*Amours*.

III   *Blois and Paris*

By 1634, Gaston was back in France, dividing his time between Blois and Paris. Shortly thereafter—certainly no later than 1636— Tristan was again a member of his household. Tristan had always loved the theater, as he readily admitted in *Le Page disgracié*, but now he seized his first opportunity to become truly involved. Frequenting the various Paris theaters, particularly the Théâtre du Marais which his friend Mondory had just established, he quickly set to work and, in 1636, his first play, *La Mariane*, became the hit of the season, a preeminence it maintained for some time, equalling in prestige and success Corneille's famous *Le Cid*. Obviously spending more time in Paris than in Blois—as did Gaston, particularly during the winter, the heart of the "season"—Tristan sought to repeat the success of his first play with a second one, but *La Panthée*, performed in 1637, did not live up to his expectations and deservedly failed.

Returning to his purely lyrical tendencies, Tristan brought out in relatively quick succession *Les Amours*, an expansion of *Les Plaintes d'Acante* (1638); *La Lyre* (1641), a collection of occasional and salon poetry, much of which had been written earlier; and several lengthy single poems. Further demonstrating his versatility, he also published a collection of letters (1642), many of them gems of pastoral fiction, *Le Page disgracié* (1643), and probably *Principes de Cosmographie* (1637), a learned work of disputed authorship. Though most of these works will be discussed at length in due time, one of their aspects—the autobiographical—is worthy of mention here.

Parallels between Tristan's plays and his life are difficult to establish.[6] On the other hand, it is easy to see them in his prose— especially in his letters and biographical novel—and in both erotic and occasional poetry. In his erotic poems, he does not "write of the burning of Troy,"[7] but simply of the tears in which he drowns. In the occasional poetry, he frequently decries the unhappy fate of the courtier; but while in previous collections the pessimism was unabated, in works such as *La Lyre*, the anguish is not without respite:

> Comme on voit après les frimas
> Dont l'hiver glace nos climats,

> La douceur du printemps renaître,
> Mes jours sortiront de leur nuit.[8]

Ambition seems a ridiculous lure (p. 115), nobility an accident of birth that does not help one to avoid problems and faults (pp. 76-77), but life is still worth living for all that.

And live it fully Tristan did indeed. By the end of 1643, with Louis XIII dead and Gaston Lieutenant-Governor of the realm, Tristan gave his third tragedy, *La Mort de Sénèque*, to the Illustre Théâtre, Molière's troupe. Its success was shortlived, but quite intense, if one is to judge by the number of editions that came out in quick succession. In 1644, Tristan produced his only tragi-comedy, *La Folie du sage* and, within a few months, another tragedy, *La Mort de Chrispe*. As the dedicatory epistles of these plays indicate, Gaston may still have been the titular lord of Tristan, but the latter was seeking greener pastures. Gaston, as I have stated previously, did not worry too much about paying his servants, and Tristan, ill and poor, was ever trying to find a more generous Maecenas. *La Folie* was dedicated to Madame, Gaston's wife; *La Mort de Sénèque* to the Duc de Saint-Aignan. When, in September, 1644, Tristan gave *Chrispe* to the comedians, he was still in Gaston's employ. When the play was published the following July, Tristan dedicated it to his new mistress, the Duchesse de Chaulnes.

IV *The last years*

> Je vois que Gaston m'abandonne
> . . . .
> Il faut dans ce malheur, que mon espoir s'adresse
> A la plus charmante Maîtresse
> Qui se puisse vanter de la faveur des Cieux.[9]

Gaston had abandoned him before. Now he seems to have dismissed him altogether. Tristan became the "chevalier d'honneur" of the Duchesse de Chaulnes, but not for long. When, late in 1645, his mistress left Paris for the Auvergne region, Tristan begged leave not to follow her, citing the worsening condition of his lungs as ample reason (*Vers héroïques*, p. 321). And so the poet who loved his freedom so much, who so deplored the fact that most of his life had been spent in the service of others, "faisant le chien couchant auprès d'un grand Seigneur,"[10] had to seek refuge at the feet of yet another noble lord, Henry II, Duc de Guise. The latter, however, was imprisoned by the Spaniards during an expedition to Naples, and Tristan found himself once again without a patron. It is possible that he found a temporary haven once more in Gaston's household; it is certain that he tried to win the favors of Christina of Sweden, but without success.

Perhaps moved by sincere sentiments of piety, more likely because he sensed a lucrative endeavor, Tristan compiled *L'Office de la Sainte Vierge*, a collection of poems intersperced with prose, brought out in 1646, obviously with haste. *Osman*, another tragedy, was performed in 1647, though not printed until after the poet's death. With de Guise in Naples, Tristan brought out his *Vers héroïques* (1648), a collection of occasional poems reflecting an entire life spent as a courtier, and dedicated it to Saint-Aignan, once again without visible results. The following year, 1649, brought better fortune, as the French Academy finally opened its doors to Tristan; but the clouds continued to predominate in his firmament: by 1651, he was again alone, in abject poverty, with his consumption gaining ground on him relentlessly.

In 1652, de Guise returned from Naples and Tristan found asylum in his rich town house. Tristan, despite his deteriorating lungs, found a certain peace and quiet there and brought out, in relatively short order, *Amarillis*, a reworking of Rotrou's pastoral *La Célimène*, and *Le Parasite*, a rowdy and vivacious comedy. When de Guise left briefly for a second Neapolitan expedition, Tristan celebrated his glorious feats—it took a great poet to see them as such—in his last long occasional poem, *La Renommée*. But time—and his health— were running out. His work on the translations of the hymns of the Roman Breviary, and on the "Oriental" novel, *La Coromène*, was interrupted by his death on September 7, 1655.[11] He was buried in the church of Saint-Jean-en-Grève which was destroyed during the Revolution.

CHAPTER 2

Prose

I General Considerations and Minor Works

FEW authors of the seventeenth century can claim Tristan L'Hermite's versatility. None achieved his level of success in as many different arenas. For the stage, he wrote tragedies, a tragi-comedy, a comedy, and a pastoral; he also wrote libretti for ballets and lyrics for court songs. His poetry ranges from stately odes to silly ditties and banal prefatory poems. But it is perhaps in the realm of prose that he demonstrated the greatest versatility, or at least the broadest range of interest and knowledge, for here, quality is not always a noteworthy part of the product.

Le Page disgracié, a story of his youth in which fact and fiction are inseparably intertwined, is one of the best picaresque novels of the day. His *Lettres*, which give us a wealth of information and insights into the man and his times, are much more than socio-historic documents: they are literary works of undeniable merit and extremely varied tone. His *Carte du Royaume d'Amour*,[1] perhaps a vestige of his now lost novel *La Coromène*, is a description of the land of love such as could be found in nearly every *précieux* novel of the time, witty, mundane, and not without psychological perspicacity. His *Principes de cosmographie*, a free translation of a work by the great mathematician François Viète, shows the extent of his eclecticism and of his intellectual appetite. The *Plaidoyers historiques*, which have been ascribed by some to his brother, are of scant literary merit, but again show the breadth of Tristan's interests and capabilities.

Many of Tristan's writings have autobiographic overtones, or are blatantly autobiographical. Poems, in spite of their conventionality and artifice, are frequently deeply personal, as I hope to demonstrate, and the heroes and heroines of many of his plays are often barely disguised interpreters of Tristan's personal feelings. But it is in

19

the letters and in his only extant novel that he shed the most direct light on his own person and personality. It is therefore proper to begin with these, though I personally do not consider them as worthy of attention as either the poems or the plays. Before doing so, however, it might be well to say a very few words about the *Plaidoyers* and the *Principes*.

Whereas most of the works of Tristan are dedicated to powerful lords and ladies, his *Plaidoyers historiques*, an adaptation of the *Epitomes de cent histoires tragiques* by the Flemish author Alexandre van den Busche, were dedicated to Tristan's own cousin, Louis-François de Caumartin, whose family, like Tristan's, was closely associated with the awakening social conscience of the times. Long before La Bruyère or Voltaire,[2] Tristan demonstrated an awareness of the misery of the lower classes, which he presented with perspicacity, incisiveness, and a compassion totally absent from the original Flemish work. The very choice of the "plaidoyers" he reworked is indicative: out of one hundred, Tristan kept barely more than one-third and added one wholly original one; and the vast majority of these deal with victims of social, political, or judicial structures.

The style of the pleas is generally rhetorical and dull, but when the author becomes involved in the moral issues, it can become very terse and combative: "There is no law more unjust or more pernicious than one which is not equal for all" (Plaid. XI), a daring statement well ahead of its time. Tristan is most eloquent when he discourses against the venality of certain offices or when he is pleading causes of the defenseless. The social themes occasionally discerned in *Le Page disgracié*, in his plays—particularly those dealing with power (and its obligations or abuses)—and in many of his occasional and autobiographical poems, form here the nucleus of a work which, for better or worse, is more of a social than a literary document. It grants us rare glimpses into Tristan the individual, Tristan the victim of an oppressive society, and for this reason deserves to have its most telling passages anthologized and brought to the attention of a larger public. But in its entirety, it is too burdened by an overly verbose rhetoric to encourage any but the most dedicated readers.

The *Principes de cosmographie* is a curious manual divided into three basic parts. The "Traité de la sphère" is a treatise expounding the geocentric theory of the universe—five years after the publication of Galileo's *Dialogo* and nearly a century after that of the *De revolutionibus* of Copernicus![3] The second part of the book, entitled "Eléments de géographie," is little more than a catalogue, a gazeteer with terse comments that mix fact and fancy as literary, historic, or mythologic references are tied to diverse localities. Descriptions range from the colorful (Mt. Hekla: "unendingly belches fire") to the arbitrary (Greenland: "Nothing of note except the monastery of St. Thomas, where spring reigns eternal," or concerning Lampedusa, one of the Pelagian Islands: "Famous for the miracle that takes place in its chapel"). The last part, dubbed "Eléments d'astronomie," deals as much with astrology and the effect of heavenly bodies on humans as with astronomy proper. In view of Tristan's thoughts of how his own life was ordered by these bodies—a subject to be discussed at length in a later chapter—here is perhaps the most interesting part of the opus.

II Le Page disgracié

Le Page disgracié is an intriguing mixture of novelistic invention and autobiographic narrative and meditation. Many critics have treated it as a more or less reliable relation of the events of Tristan's youth, going so far as to base biographical sketches on it; others have detected large borrowings, particularly from Italian *conteurs* and Spanish novelists. Even some of the musings of the young page are taken directly from Alemán's *Guzman de Alfarache,* the great picaresque novel of the turn of the century. With equal frequency, the book has been called a Realistic novel, and indeed, it is not devoid of Realistic elements—in the description of life behind the scenes at court, on the battlefield, on the highways and byways, the inns and ale houses, in the homes of the upper and middle classes—but "Realism" must here be redefined, for Tristan relied on suggestion and hints, on terse—nearly brutally so—cameos, not on the endless descriptive passages to which nineteenth-century "Realists" have accustomed us. But in spite of these elements, *Le Page* is not a Realistic novel, as Antoine Adam quite rightly points out,[4] for Tristan, far from depicting life as it was, had as his main object to be "vraisemblable et divertissant"—to use the words of his contemporary, Sorel—that is to say, Tristan had to be verisimilar and amusing. The semblance of truth allows the reader to accept what may, after all, be but wishful thinking and vicarious thrills. Antoine Adam deplores this situation which makes the book so hard to define by asking: part memoir, part novel, part invention, and part borrowing. Exactly what is it? It no doubt defies easy classification, but it is quite effective for all that.

I believe that while it might be interesting to separate the autobiographical from the invented (or borrowed) elements so as to know more about the life of Tristan, in so far as the *Le Page* as a work of art is concerned to do so would be counterproductive. As in so many of his other endeavors in all possible genres, Tristan worked very hard here to intertwine dream and reality, or better still, physical and psychological reality. *Le Page* might best be considered not a relating of events that took place during the youth of its author, but that same time of youth as the older man would have liked it to be. This of course sheds valuable light on the personality of the author, but it also allows us to view the work as an entity with intrinsic, artistic merits.

In the second, posthumous edition of *Le Page*, dedicated to the Duc de Verneuil, one of the early masters of the young page, "keys" were given, decoding names of people and places, and thus giving the work a better historic perspective. Such revelations, however, do not necessarily serve the literary purpose of the book: the ambiguity— and tension—between history and invention is best left unresolved.

If *Le Page* is not a Realistic novel, what is it? Should it be categorized? Can it in fact be? I believe that, with certain reservations, *Le Page* can, and that for reasons which I hope will become obvious, should. Because the page rushes from incident to incident, from locale to locale, we never get to know the people he encounters. They remain strangers whose single exposed facet is the one required to reflect the page's own traits. Only he is known, with all his aspirations and weaknesses. To better isolate that phenomenon, to give it a name—a process that first requires analysis and identification—is, I am convinced, to better understand the work and its author.

Everything about the title is an indication, a warning: *page* ("servitude"); *disgracié* ("misfortune"); the entire subtitle (*Où l'on voit de vifs caractères d'hommes de tous tempéraments et de toutes professions*), everything bespeaks the picaresque. The *pìcaro* is a "dépaysé," an exile in every land, in fact and in spirit; such is the case of the page. To describe Tristan's unstable protagonist is to sum up the characteristics of the *pìcaro* as outlined by Claudio Guillén[5]: introspective and shrewd, sometime philosopher, the page-*pìcaro* changes according to circumstances—perhaps the main attribute rescuing him from comicality. He is either orphaned or torn from his family by need or force of events. Thus "dépaysé", he must face the world with whatever is at his disposal, to live not *in* a society, but rather on the edges of it, or off it entirely.

The picaresque genre, as described by Guillén, could have been patterned after Tristan's *Page.* The picaresque novel being autobiographic, or pseudo such, the narration allows not only a double vision (object-subject), but a manipulation of the distance between the inner person and the public image. As a result, only some aspects of the *pìcaro*'s life are brought to bear; the narrator freely and subjectively selects these, as he judges and selects as models some of the people he meets while rejecting others. As the *pìcaro* comes into contact with people, with entire social strata, these are commented on, but from the "coulisses" as it were, with an emphasis on material things, and only in so far as they affect the wanderer who is the sole link between people or episodes.

Forced to wander in a crass society, this protagonist is led to compare the drives of his innermost being with the modalities of his precarious life. As he views this *décalage*, he frequently waxes ironic, a reflection of an inuring process that takes place (and of which he is also conscious). Nowhere is this more obvious than in the last paragraph of the opus in which he announces to his friend a sequel that was never written—that could not be written, since he was reentering the life he had left to become a *pìcaro*. As the narrator tells his friend why, henceforth, he will want as little intercourse with his fellow men as possible, a sublime irony becomes apparent: the court that becomes his haven is precisely that element of society from which he originally fled, and in which he still sees the same characteristics that engendered his flight. He knows that to survive in it, he will have to be even more clever, more dissimulating than ever before, as well as pursue dealings that will give him "disgust for all the professions of the world" and "hatred for many diverse societies." In other words, in retrospect the narrator has found that court to be a mixture of "honnêteté" and "ridicule," a material haven as equally inimical to his inner being as ever were the milieus the page traversed in his peregrinations.

Two episodes of *Le Page* are usually highlighted and discussed as being of primary importance; the first involves the author's encounter with the alchemist who, touched by the naive devotion of the young man, promises him fame and fortune, happiness and health; from then on, the page lives in the hope that some day this will come to pass. This hope gives a sense of direction to his efforts to wrench himself free from the slavery of daily exigencies. The other episode concerns the idyllic love affair he has in England, which ends so dramatically when he is accused of being a poisonner and must flee. Once again, he has his hope dashed and his happiness destroyed, but the memory of this intense experience remains etched in his heart and mind. It is the vision of a paradise lost that will remain unchanged, even when the older and wiser (and more bitter) narrator handles it. The old alchemist and the young Englishwoman have given him the strength to struggle, but how the struggle has affected him is best revealed in the aforementioned last paragraph of the novel:

Dear Thirinte, this is how ends the eighteenth or nineteenth year of my life. Excuse the puerilities of one of that age, and do me the honor of readying your attention for the remainder. You will note an assemblage of many things more agreeable and which will be better suited to your humor. You will hear of adventures more virtuous and ridiculous whose diversity can relieve diverse melancholies. I will make you understand the disgust that I have for all the professions of the world, and what has made me hate many diverse societies. It is in these two volumes that follow that you will become acquainted with the apprenticeship that I made in the knowledge of men, and how wrong or right I am to want their company but rarely. (Bk. II, Ch. 55.)

As is the case in any other autobiographical work, the author of *Le Page* offers himself as a spectacle; as *pìcaro*, he travels through a world whose main function is to serve as a spectacle for his eyes. This world is one of stark realism, and the author is far from squeamish;[6] the events that take place may or may not be true; his reactions to them, like the events themselves, are as he wishes them to be, or to appear to be.[7] At the outset, when the young page plays with his still younger royal master, whose immunity transforms the "forbidden games" of the page into quite harmless and ordinary royal pastimes, the frontier between the commonplace and the adventurous dream is given a new meaning. The prince becomes symbolic of the dream, the escape from reality and contingencies, the means for Tristan to enjoy, however vicariously, what otherwise would be quite out of the question. But one day the dichotomy and its injustice become too much for the page; in a violent movement of revolt, he draws his sword, sheds blood, and tears the veil of the dream. From then on, the world will be the stage for Tristan the actor-director-playwright. Tristan writes a novel about a young man who lived a novel, using the world as a backdrop for his picaresque adventures and wanderings. But even in this part of the novel, the thirst for the forbidden, the vicious and the vitiated, is manifest as the page constantly runs afoul of law and society, constantly plagued by memories of past misfortunes and apprehensions about the future that mar his passing joys.

Subjacent throughout the book, the interplay of mature introspection and memory becomes apparent in the last chapter, where the narrator reveals himself and his function—as distinct from the "narratee," the subject—and shows the evolution of Tristan from subject-page to the more mature (and disillusioned) author. Throughout the novel, there is evident a pattern of attempts to escape the realities of life by peregrinations and dreams, or attempts to find an ideal, frustrated to be sure but with a frustration that is palliated by the writer creating a refuge for his illusions (as the writer establishes new worlds, he gives new hopes to the wanderer). This search for happiness, by means of created dreams that combat the bleakness of reality, lies at the core of the work. As this search is constantly frustrated, ideals are lost, bitterness grows (or at least a despondency and willingness to abandon oneself to the adverse stars that dictate such a fate), and the prevailing mood changes from ever-renewed optimism to melancholy. The search for ideals gives way to a new mode, a struggle for survival in order to enjoy the days as they come for what they may bring. But, the importance of the last paragraph goes beyond that: the page, however wise he may have become, appears naive when compared to the narrator (who characterizes the page as naive), warning of further disenchantment and total alienation.

What is not stated in this last paragraph, but becomes very obvious in the last chapters of the novel, is that the spectacle of the world intertwined with the presentation of the *picaro*-as-spectacle takes on new proportions. The wanderer ceases to be truly central as his anecdotal recollections become more and more focused on events external to his own miserable state. Chronology ceases to be a factor as he ceases to be the major link between episodes: he is himself no longer the central spectacle, but a less and less significant part of the spectacle that is the world. Like the *picaro* of the Spanish novels—or of later French attempts such as *Gil Blas*—he is tossed by fate, driven by circumstances, sometimes catalyst, sometimes victim, sometimes barely spectator, ingratiating himself but never quite finding either his niche—or himself. Once he has reached that stage where the author-actor has become mere spectator, the *raison d'être* of the autobiographical novel ceases to be valid, and the work abruptly ends. If the novel is seen as the mere story of a man, then this abrupt ending makes no sense. If, on the contrary, we see that Tristan was primarily concerned with a value or values, then the recession of the protagonist into the background is legitimate and must herald the end of the narrative. That is the strength of the opus. It is also its weakness: introspection in such a work is deceptive—does it emanate from Tristan the page or Tristan the mature author? In fact, Tristan plays too much with this notion, thus destroying, or at least weakening, the narrative texture so essential to a picaresque novel.

III   Les Lettres mêlées

Collections of letters were very popular in Tristan's days, and letters were considered a literary genre worthy of cultivation and admiration.[8] There is no doubt that Tristan intended to take advantage of the vogue, and that the book was published in haste. The rapidity of composition (the *privilège* is of January 10, 1642, the *achevé* five days later) led to numerous typographical errors and some very sloppy printing. But critics have made too much of this; the typographical errors are many and the likelihood of authorial opportunism is undeniable, but the content and the quality have nothing to do with either. Most of these letters, in spite of what N.-M. Bernardin has said[9] are intended for public consumption, and quite carefully composed. They were obviously ready for publication well before the occasion presented itself (the oncoming marriage of Elisabeth de Choiseul-Praslin, a protector of Tristan and an amateur of letters). The wedding present, dedicated to her, though hastily printed, had been ready for some time.

Like most letter writers of his day, Tristan knew that to a public avid of the written word, letters tended to become public property, open to general perusal and judgment. The craftsmanship of these letters is far from even, but it is nonetheless quite good. Many show great ingenuity; others are platitudinous in every way. All, however, like *Le Page disgracié*, give us a precious insight into Tristan the man, the courtier, and the writer. He makes frequent and interesting allusions to events in his life, to the state of his finances and of his health—both always bad—to his religious sentiments and family ties. His comments on friendship are particularly touching and illuminating. The author even airs his publication problems as he complains of the Walloon printers, ignorant "barbarians" who butchered the edition of his *Plaintes* (Letter 86).

Like *Le Page*, these letters are also a strange mixture of autobiographical procedures, alternating as they do expressions of innermost feelings and highly sophisticated—and intricately crafted— elaborations of commonplaces on such feelings.[10] The letter, as I have said, was considered a far from negligible genre at the time, and Jean Ogier de Gombauld said that it was for prose what the sonnet was for poetry.[11] It was expected to be composed according to strict rules derived from an illustrious tradition of rhetoric.

It is, therefore, of the utmost importance to view these letters in the context of a tradition of epistolary composition. It must be noted that Tristan divided his collection according to the function of his epistles (dedicatory letters, letters of consolation, love letters, "heroic" letters, and, finally, an olio of "mixed" letters which loaned its title to the collection as a whole). It must also be noted, however, that another division is possible if not necessary, that between "real" letters—that is to say, letters which, before publication and public consumption, were meant for and probably sent to or presented to real addressees—and letters which were penned as literary devices meant only for readers of a collection. Both represent conscious literary efforts to be appreciated by a wide public; but the initial impetus or *raison d'être* of the letter perforce colors its composition. The "Dedicatory" letters are, of course, "real." So are most of the letters collected under the last rubric of "lettres mêlées." The bulk of the rest are not, and while they reveal no less of their author's travails and thoughts, they do so in a quite different way.

The nine dedicatory letters in the collection—seven are so labelled, one heads the book, and letter 63 originally accompanied his "Maison d'Astrée"—follow a definite pattern in the rhetorical tradition of the demonstrative type of literature. Their principal function is to praise the addressee, to give protestations of total devotion and subservience on the part of the writer—who must admit insufficiencies in both himself and his work, the acceptance of the latter by the addressee proving not the merit of the work but the generosity of the addressee. This is, of course, but one of many virtues, all of which are carefully catalogued by the writer, before being proven: first by genetic considerations (the illustrious ancestry), then by deeds (real or, in the case of a youthful addressee, projected), and, finally, by enumerating the "monuments" (verbal, written, or concrete) erected by the contemporaries (and no doubt to be erected by posterity). After this enumeration, the writer suggests that if the addressee accepts this unworthy tribute, it is out of kindness, and if the tribute is brief, this is so not because its author lacks for imagination or subject matter, but because he is afraid that praise, however deserved it may be, can only offend the modest addressee. Tristan's letters all follow this mode. They are carefully composed, conventional, and invariably banal.

The letters of consolation were also expected to follow rather rigid guidelines and to have two goals: to praise the departed and to exhort the bereaved to be brave and find solace. Here again, Tristan's letters appear conventional and trite. The fault no doubt lies in the manuals which dictated the form and formulae proper to consolations, going so far as to specify the exact approach to be used for various degrees of sorrow.

Thus, the first letter, beginning as it does with a scolding of the mourner, berating her for not finding solace in time, is not unusually harsh or out of place. On the contrary, it adheres very closely to the rules of the genre, even in the specifics of the scolding and the advice that follows. As Catherine Grisé points out in her introduction to the letters, the rules—particularly of *bienséance*—dictated that letters of consolation follow the prescribed pattern: first, some general reflections on death (time being a balm, excessive sorrow equated with self-hate, death as inescapable and logical) followed by famous examples and definitions, "all syllogisms leading to the same conclusion: one must cease complaining."[12] Then follow arguments centered around the idea that continued sorrowing will have adverse effects on both the mourner and those that surround her. Finally, with recourse to the "demonstrative" rhetorical devices, the author exhorts the mourner to take advantage of her exemplary nature and to give an example of firmness and courage to those that follow her. All this is to be found without deviation in all the letters of consolation, following the rules of usage and the dictates of the savants, and the only original contribution of Tristan is in the stylistic details, Tristanian signatures such as the generous use of his favorite metaphors, a more fruitful discussion of which will be taken up in the chapters dealing with his poetry.

Unlike the preceding, the heroic letters are purely artificial, that is to say, that the addressee is fictitious (as is the supposed writer). Here again, we are dealing with a highly conventional genre, one that can be traced back to Ovid, but whose more immediate predecessors were the writings of the Italians of the preceding generation.[13] The heroes in question may be legendary, historic, or taken from recent literature. Like the women of Ovid's *Heroides,* they write not only of love, but also of momentous events or situations. In these letters, the heroic writer tries to convince the no less heroic addressee of his or her love, or pleads a case for same. Catherine Grisé likens these letters to the monologues of the great classical tragedies, since the letter is provoked "by a dramatic and serious situation," but, she adds, "the situation does not change and there is no dramatic action between characters: everything occurs in the heart of the sender."[14] That is not entirely true, since a monologue is, by definition, intended for no ears but those of the spectator, while the heroic letter, again by definition, is intended to convince a specific addressee, forestalling his or her rebuttals and countering whatever arguments the writer thinks might be presented.

These letters are frequently dramatic—though conventionally so—but Tristan goes well beyond the genre's mediocrity: "How dare you accuse me of imprudence when I do not wish to yield to your unbridled desires? And you take upon yourself to teach me, you who have lost your reason? . . . Though you may try to make me feel your indignation if I refuse to love you, I fear your love more than your threats" (Letter 60). The subject is taken from Ariosto (*Orlando furioso,* canto 21), as are so many of the basic ideas in this tirade by a woman in love; but Tristan has added a very personal cachet, the dramatization of the woman's moral indignation, which "transforms into a discursive style the succinct narrative of Ariosto."[15] As is common with such letters, Tristan sets up straw men which the writer can knock over most readily. The king of Peru says to Pizarro (Letter 61):

I cannot imagine how people as insatiable of gold and as cruel as you could be either faithful or truthful. You assure me of the mercy of your gods; I do not doubt it, since they allow men as wicked as you to survive. You exalt the great possessions and virtue of your king, and that I cannot believe: if he were as rich as you make him out to be, he would not send you so far and at such great risks to seek what he has in abundance at home; and if he were such a lover of justice, he would not give permission to his subjects to rob and kill those who have done him no harm.

As a result, these heroic letters are some of the most interesting in the collection, both for their dramatic impact and for the generous use of the themes and contrasts that pervade Tristan's best poems.

Like their heroic counterparts, the "Lettres amoureuses" are wholly fictitious, but with an added twist: whereas the heroic letter is written by and to a specific person (fictitious or not), the addressees of the love letters, like the sentiments involved, are mere abstractions. The themes, metaphors, and striking conceits that permeate these letters are, therefore, the same as those we shall encounter in the erotic poetry of Tristan, though perforce less refined: "I have told you that these dealings were like a sea on which your reputation risked to be wrecked, and you write that you indeed foresee that danger and are sorry that you embarked. Well, my cute one, if such is the case, that you fear this peril however little, and that my advice may seem useful, the anchor has not yet been raised, the wind has not filled the sails, you are still in the harbor, and have only to disembark" (Letter 28). Such is not always the case, however, and in letter 35, the ingenuity of the lover is well matched by the refinement and artifice of his language, as he details to his mistress an entire code of secret signals thanks to which they will be able to communicate under the noses of her vigilant relatives.

These letters, then, are of great interest for the light they shed on the personality and feelings of the author. They are equally valuable for students of Tristan's craftsmanship who can see in them variations of themes elaborated elsewhere. Several of them are very good; most of them offer little to redeem the banality that permeates them. They show another aspect of Tristan's multifaceted endeavors while adding little to his glory.

CHAPTER 3

Poetry:The Individual

I General Considerations

TRISTAN frequently hoarded his poems for later publication: some of the poems published in his last anthology are works of his youth. With the notable exception of certain circumstantial works, a dating of his verses is thus virtually impossible, and a chronological study—however desirable or undesirable it might be—out of the question. Yet those poems that are patently the product of his later years have a decidedly different quality, darker in coloring, more personal in tone, eschewing the *précieux* and marinistic devices he so loved to exhibit in his earlier years. There will thus, in the following pages, be some distinction made between the "early" and the "late" manner of Tristan; but this does not mean that one must look for a revolutionary break. With this in mind, I have thought it advisable to divide the discussion of Tristan's poetry into broad thematic categories, immense—and admittedly clumsy—tapestries on which circumstancial poems would have to be more or less frequently and artificially grafted.

By the same token, though some poems may appear more "personal" than others, it is not only difficult, but dangerous, to think of a "real" Tristan as opposed to a "façade." Rather, the reader must see that in the seventeenth century, artifice and sincerity were not considered opposites. As Philip Wadsworth has so keenly noted, "the word 'artifice,' in its best and broadest sense, denotes skillfully executed workmanship, the technical resourcefulness which enters into any work of art. It does not deny the possibility of sincerity; indeed it may contribute to the truth and genuineness with which an artist reveals his personality." In Tristan, particularly in his early poetry, this "fondness for ingenious literary devices" goes hand in hand with "an expression of strong emotion which seems to spring directly from his heart."[1]

31

One of the most "artificial" of Tristan's works, the "Plaintes d'Acante," has such convincing marks of sincerity that critics were fooled for nearly three centuries: everyone thought that Tristan had written these lover's plaints for himself, bemoaning his own amorous hardships. Only in 1937 did Eugénie Droz discover the original manuscript which proved that Tristan had written these lines for another.[2] Yet this discovery, so important for our understanding of Tristan, should not blind us to the fact—obvious for three centuries—that in these soulful lines, it is indeed a lover speaking. Tristan, no less a lover than his patron, expressed his own innermost feelings. The words of love of one man fit the needs of another, the one who had commissioned them. Why should this detract from their sincerity? To have these feelings accepted by a cultured lady, Tristan had to couch them in ingenious terms, but for all their preciosity and artifice, they are no less real and heartfelt.[3] Critics speak of Marinistic, Petrarchistic, *précieux* tendencies in Tristan's work, and anthologists have even left out the last quatrains of the magnificent "Promenoir des deux amants" because of their artificiality, never realizing, as so perspicaciously did Amédée Carriat, that Tristan had gone well beyond the Petrarchist tradition, that he had found, through metaphors, puns, antitheses, and concetti, the cultivated intonation that best touches a cultured heart.[4]

It is therefore of the utmost importance for the modern reader not only to analyze and appreciate the marvelous craftsmanship of Tristan, what Philip Wadsworth has called "his ingenuity, his theatricality, his use of contrast and surprise, his fondness for movement and metamorphosis, his emphasis or exaggeration,"[5] but to see that this very craftmanship is the signature of the man and that, without the appreciation of the one, there is no understanding of the other. Ingenuity—that primal attribute of preciosity, making itself manifest via periphrasis and metaphor—never completely hides the underlying sensitivity of the poet and of the man. Part of the game played by the gentility—"L'honnête homme est celui qui ne se pique de rien"—is not to completely hide the game, but to show that it is precisely that, that both writer and reader know it, and that they both knowingly play it. It is precisely this consciousness that saves many of the extreme periphrases and metaphors from being ridiculous: the feverish beauty being described as a morning sun unable to rise, for instance, leads more to an appreciation of a game well played than to the thought of ridiculous failure or excess.

When Tristan plays that game, the deliberate impression of naïveté in no way eclipses our awareness of great technical skill. Sensibility and imagination are, in fact, communicated by means of technique as language is ever put to the task of conveying every nuance of perception. To better understand this total alliance of technique and sensibility, let us look at the initial stanza of "La servitude":

> Nuit fraiche, sombre, et solitaire,
>> Sainte dépositaire
> De tous les grands secrets, ou de guerre, ou d'amour,
> Nuit mère du repos, et nourrice des veilles
>> Qui produisent tant de merveilles,
> Donne moi des conseils qui soient dignes du jour.[6]

The first two lines are united by their brevity as well as their rhyme, but the forceful enjambment between lines two and three makes a single unit of the first twenty beats, to which the second hemistich of line three is added like an afterthought. Syntactically, the alexandrine might be considered to be the union of line two and the first hemistich of the next line. These first three lines, despite the punctuation, are thus a distinct unit, a separation emphasized by the recapitulative nature of the first two lines of the second half. But these two lines definitely lack something—call it equilibrium, or better yet, a sense of repose—which only the last alexandrine can supply. So it becomes apparent that if one is to speak of unity and of composition, whether in a single stanza or an entire poem, it cannot be in terms of meter or form, but with regard to a more comprehensive vision, one that encompasses the inner unity, what has been called the "higher, hidden order" of imagistic or metaphoric coherence. *Ut pictura poesis*, to be sure, but with a sensitive brush that conveys all that is hidden under the purely formal level.

II *Ego*

Gentleman in one of the most intransigent caste systems in history, Tristan was proud of his state, yet painfully aware of its implications, its duties, and those obligations never reduced by his poverty or subservient state. Seldom in this mundane and sophisticated society did a poet so readily epitomize the precarious dichotomy that must have prevailed in the hearts of all, that involving both superficial worldliness—and disquieted (and disquieting) sensitivity. Abhorring "the emotions and lowly passions of self-seeking souls" (*Amours*, "Plainte à la belle banquière"), he frequently sought in the country, with friends, the *repos* so dear to Madame de La Fayette; yet he could never think seriously of leaving a court where the behavior he decried prevailed. The justly famous "Ode à M. de Chaudebonne" speaks eloquently of his desire for peace and friendship to be enjoyed along with the simple pleasures offered by a bountiful nature, yet such declarations must perforce be juxtaposed (and tempered) with those indicating that happiness away from princely courts is impossible.

The answer to the riddle is perhaps best rendered in lines from his long poem on servitude:

> Irais-je m'abaisser en mille et mille sortes,
> Et mettre le siège à vingt portes
> Pour arracher du pain qu'on ne me tendrait pas?[7]

A free and proud spirit, Tristan hated the prostitution of his pen and of his person. As he stated in another poem, the weight of the chains borne by his Muse crippled his best lines (*Vers héroïques*, "A. M. de Voiture"); but Tristan knew, as his editor put it, that to succeed one had to be a politician, and had to spend as much time with the patrons as with the Muses (*Vers héroïques*, "Advertissement à qui lit"). Time and time again, as in "A M. de Patris," he comes back to the theme of ungrateful and unappreciative patrons. He knows that he will find vindication in posterity, but what will be the good of that? If he is the poorest of mortals, "Que sert après la mort beaucoup de renommée?"[8]

His disenchantment is made all the more apparent by the juxtaposition of the reiterated proclamations of his own worth. However frequently Tristan may refer to commonplaces such as *mors ultima ratio* or *carpe diem*, he knows that death will at least spare one monument: his poetry. Monuments may crumble, but, like Shakespeare's, his powerful rhymes will survive and, with them, the glory of those patrons whose deeds and virtues he praises (*Plaintes*, "L'Avis considérable"; *La Lyre*, "A M. de Montauron"). He knows that he cannot obtain the approval of all, and, therefore does not seek it, hoping only for the suffrage of people of taste. Thus, when a lady approves of his efforts, he is overjoyed; he begins by thanking the Muses:

> Je n'ai point de regret d'avoir suivi vos traces
> Et vous rends mille graces
> Des célestes secrets que vous m'avez appris.

The reason for this new confidence is soon made manifest:

> Et certain désormais qu'ils ont de l'excellence,
> Je puis sans insolence
> Permettre qu'un laurier me presse les cheveux.

Why? Because Sylvie has approved his efforts, as he states in a delightful conceit:

> Elle trouve en mon style une douceur extrême
> Et confesse elle même
> Que j'ai beaucoup de grâce à montrer ses rigueurs.[9]

When that necessary support fails him, or is altogether denied, then his urbanity yields to frustration and an ever-present fatalism, as demonstrated in the already cited "Ode à M. de Chaudebonne": What the stars have dictated for him cannot be denied or obviated. This is, of course, a commonplace in Renaissance and Baroque poetry, a convention to be exploited (and Tristan does full justice to the occasion). To come into the world without strength or skills, to be miserable all one's life, to pine in vain for an unyielding woman, to intrigue at court until old age and its inevitable miseries force one into retirement awaiting death; if such is the lot of man, why love life and fear death to such an extent (*Amours*, "Misère de l'homme du monde")? In *La Lyre*, this pessimism is compounded by cynicism: if man ever attains wisdom, it is only to be able to fathom his misery; if he succeeds in life, it is only to give rise to jealousy and calumny ("A M. de Saintot").

If Tristan only exploited such commonplaces, there would be little to recommend him; but he goes well beyond, impregnating the expression of the ordinary with a mood all his own. The struggle, the tension between the delicacy of expression and the intensity of feelings, is unequalled by his contemporaries. Capable of elegiacal tones—"S'il te souvient encor de ces douces atteintes" (*La Lyre*, "Orphée"—he never allows this mood to escape the yoke of reserve and prudent modesty, not even in such cries of despair as "C'est fait de mes destins." Haunted by the fragility of human fortune and the instability of all things, Tristan, like Rousseau, presents a human being to his reader, but one who suffers quietly and never forgets that he is a gentleman. Noblesse oblige.

III *The Language of Love*

"Je est un autre," said Gérard Genette speaking of the Baroque
treatment of the Narcissus theme.[10] This phrase can easily be used to
capsulize Tristan's notion of love, platonic or sexual. I have already
spoken of his discretion and reserve, personal qualities which he
demonstrated in his poetic endeavors and by which he was guided in
all his relationships. To these must be added one which he considered
of the utmost importance, one of which he was justly proud, and
which he demanded in others: faithfulness. When his brother asked
him to give up serving Gaston, a most ungrateful patron, Tristan
replied that he could not: "I would be cowardly indeed if I abandoned him during his misfortunes. Before joining him, I could have
chosen another master, but now I can have neither will nor life unless
it be to sacrifice them to his interests and to follow his fortune."[11]
Théophile de Viau, a poet abandonned by all when on trial and in
disgrace, found Tristan steadfastly at his side.

Already in "La Mer," Tristan had expressed the sense of loss at the
death of a friend. It was not until the publication of *La Lyre*, in 1641,
that a large part of an entire collection was devoted to such a topic.
Whether in jest ("A M. Ranchin") or in sorrow (numerous "consolations"), Tristan declared himself a faithful friend and hoped to find
like sentiments in others. He knew, however, that his was a
"barbarous" age, "in which a true friend is a rare treasure," especially
one that is "discreet, faithful, and worthy of his choice" ("Orphée").
He expected his friends to share his views and to consider, as he did,
that there is nothing worse than unfaithful friends" ("Plainte pour
Monsieur D. B.").

Despite the large place given to friendship in *La Lyre*, Tristan
remains principally a poet of love. Though he is not averse to
immortalizing friendship by means of his verses ("Orphée"), his real
ambition is far more personal:

> Je n'écris point ici l'embrasement de Troye
> . . . .
> J y dépeins seulement les pleurs dont je me noïe
> . . . .
> Aussi je n'attends pas que le bruit de mes vers,
> Portant ma renommée au bout de l'Univers,
> Etende ma mémoire au delà de ma vie:
> J'en veux moins acquérir d'honneur que d'amitié;

> Les autres ont dessein de donner de l'envie,
> Et le point où j'aspire est de faire pitié.[12]

With rare exceptions, the love of which Tristan speaks is one that has been crushed or frustrated. He repeatedly described the travails of love and its sorrows, rarely its pleasures. This tendency, visible from the first, becomes more and more pronounced as time goes on, so that when in a late poem he lists his woes, he states that his cup would really overflow if he were now cursed with a love or a litigation (*Vers héroïques* "Stances sur le même sujet"). However, there is evident no feeling of utter despair or great sorrow. Once again, the impression is that Tristan is here too playing a game, coping with a purely intellectual puzzle. This "intellectual fascination" (Genette, p. 564) may well betray anxieties, but it does not—by its very nature—pose any intrinsic dangers; on the contrary: the triumph over such dangers derives from their verbalization. This is perhaps why the titles of so many of Tristan's love poems sound like way stations of the *Carte de Tendre* or of his own *Carte du Royaume d'Amour*, two maps describing the roads to true love.

Games, of course, are played by rules, and it should be of no surprise to find that Tristan's erotic poetry is replete with the commonplaces then in vogue. The themes, even the specific images evoked by the poet, are easily traced to French—and even more frequently Italian—contemporaries. Metaphors dealing with the standard *blason*, i.e., the parts of the human body, however ingeniously twisted or refined by Tristan, can almost all be traced to Marino and Guarini. Thus, the hair of the beloved is described as golden waves that have robbed gold of its price, a sea in which the lover is blissfully shipwrecked; if the hair in question is tied, then the lover, once bound by it (i.e., the prisoner of love), is glad to see it bound in turn. Some of these metaphors can be extremely complex:

> Ce baiser est un sceau par qui ma vie est close;
> Et comme on peut trouver un serpent sous des fleurs,
> J'ai rencontré ma mort sur un bouton de rose.[13]

The ambiguity of the first line is further enmeshed in the deliberate *double entendre* on death in its most erotic connotation as expounded in the two closing lines.

Such verbal gymnastics can only be appreciated if the reader sees them as the emanation of an impulse to make the word equal all the tumult of the senses. This is precisely Tristan's aim, and, in poems such as "Orphée", he goes even further, making the words reproduce paintings and evoke music. The ultimate conceit, of course, is to reverse the process—and Tristan could not refuse the challenge: a marble statue can fool the viewer and make him think that it is alive, merely contemplative or temporarily frozen in motion; an unfeeling lady can just as readily be turned into marble, and entire groups can be metamorphosed into statues (*Les Amours,* "La Pamoison," "L'Accident merveilleux," "La Fortune de l'hermaphrodite").

If this sensuous tumultuousness is to be evoked, the poet cannot rely exclusively on intellectual games. His lines must have a musicality that conjures up Orphic spirits, and his descriptions must have a plasticity to delight the mind's eye. It is here that Tristan, not content with imitating Marino, embues the metaphors of that Italian master with a warm sensuality all his own.

I have already cited the last lines of "L'Extase d'un baiser," whose sounds are so evocative of the lover's death. That same final quietus is preceded by lines that bespeak the horror of the realization of impending death and, here again, Tristan perfectly allied the music with the meaning. Note the harshness of the sounds (especially when contrasted with the already cited "Ce baiser est un sceau par qui ma vie est close"):

> Mais tout mon sang s'altère, une brûlante fièvre
> Me ravit la couleur et m'ôte la raison;

outburst leading to the quiet of understanding:

> Cieux! J'ai pris à la fois sur cette belle lèvre
> D'un céleste nectar et d'un mortel poison.[14]

But if the exciting moments of passion are so successfully translated into verse by Tristan, it is first and foremost because of the plasticity—though a sensuous and warm one—that permeates his lines.

Critics have frequently dismissed "La Belle gueuse" as merely imitative of Claudio Achillini's "Bellissima Mendica." It is an imitation, to be sure, but a masterful one that goes well beyond the model. The eyes shining like sapphires, the spilling hair likened to a shower of gold, all the specific attributes give a visual dimension to a description of youthful vitality and beauty. It is however with two other poems, the early "Les Cheveux blonds" and "La Belle esclave maure," that this art of depiction is best illustrated. Here is, in its entirety, one of the first of many poems devoted by Tristan to the hair of the beloved, a part of the *blason* which seems to haunt him and to permeate his erotic musings:

> Fin Or, de qui le prix est sans comparaison
> Clairs rayons d'un Soleil, douce et subtile trame
> Dont la molle étendue a des ondes de flamme
> Où l'Amour mille fois a noyé ma raison.
>
> Beau poil, votre franchise est une trahison.
> Faul-il qu'en vous montrant, vous me cachiez madame?
> N'était-ce pas assez de captiver mon âme
> Sans retenir ainsi ce beau corps en prison?
>
> Mais o doux flots dorés, votre orgueil se rabaisse;
> Sous la dextérité d'une main qui vous presse,
> Vous allez comme moi, perdre la liberté.
>
> Et j'ai le bien de voir une fois en ma vie
> Qu'en liant le beau poil qui me tient arrêté,
> On ôte la franchise à qui me l'a ravie.[15]

Color, texture, light, all the elements of depiction are there, transforming the verbal metaphor into a Rubenesque canvas.

Here, now, is the second example, "La Belle esclave maure," a mutation of a cliché that was itself becoming commonplace, perhaps one of the earliest examples in Western society of the notion that "black is beautiful":

> Beau Monstre de nature, il est vrai, ton visage
> Est noir au dernier point, mais beau parfaitement:
> Et l'Ebène poli qui te sert d'ornement
> Sur le plus blanc ivoire emporte l'avantage.
>
> O merveille divine inconnue à notre âge!
> Qu'un objet ténébreux luise si clairement;
> Et qu'un charbon éteint, brûle plus vivement
> Que ceux qui de la flamme entretiennent l'usage!
>
> Entre ces noires mains je mets ma liberté;
> Moi qui fut invincible à toute autre Beauté,

Une More m'embrase, une Esclave me dompte.

Mais cache-toi Soleil, toi qui viens de ces lieux
D'où cet Astre est venu, qui porte pour ta honte
La nuit sur son visage et le jour dans ses yeux.[16]

There is no need here to go into a detailed analysis of the obvious puns and oxymora, and of their startling effects. What must be pointed out, however, is that no matter how different this poem may seem from the one previously cited, the effect of the central metaphor is the same—the creation of an erotic tableau, one embued with its own distinctive ambience.

This brings us to a question basic to all poetry, but particularly important in Tristan's erotic verses. A key metaphor, by its simplicity and its transparency, can easily "explain" or communicate what an elaborate attempt at description could not transmit. If a metaphor remains etched in the reader's mind, even after the logical structure of an argument or a minute physical or psychological description— without which that metaphor would never have assumed its ascendency—has been forgotten, is this not precisely because it remains the key thanks to which we have "captured" the message (whether it be archetypal and familiar, or revolutionary and original)?[17]

In that sense, far from being vague, such a metaphor is precise in that it distills an entire situation or emotion to isolate or highlight the one component, the one trait thanks to which the reader can capture the message and make it his own. Tristan—or for that matter, any poet—uses metaphors to convey precise psychological notions when, face to face with what the seventeenth century called the undefinable *je ne sais quoi*, the communicative effectiveness of conventional, literal language is in doubt. Under such circumstances, the metaphor is no longer A figure of rhetoric, but THE figure, THE means by which the poet transmits his message and demonstrates his originality and individuality. It is the means by which he penetrates his subject and reveals its most diverse psychological and sensory ramifications.

In any given realm, metaphors can only enrich the language. But they do more, and this is where Tristan is such a master of his trade: relying on the cognitive respectibility of his metaphors, Tristan deliberately erased the lines of demarcation between the literal and the figurative—i.e., the blond hair and the golden waves—creating a climate of coexistence. As the reason can drown in the billowy waves, so can the senses be overwhelmed by the texture and perfume of the hair. Thus, Tristan allows the reader to fully share his vision and sensations as the *blason* of the feminine body becomes, like the countryside of the Symbolists, an *étât d'âme*, a Baudelairian "temple in which living pillars sometimes allow confused words to come forth, where man passes through forests of symbols . . . [and where] perfumes, colors and sounds echo each other."[18]

CHAPTER 4

Poetry: Society

I Court and Servitude

"IT is an excellent art, to know how to feign well," says Dina to Mariane in Tristan's first play (*La Mariane*, 352). As I have already stated, it is an art which Tristan abhorred, but he knew, nevertheless, that to eke out a living as a gentleman who wished to make his way in the republic of letters, there was but one place for him—a princely or royal court—no matter what his private feelings about such a life might be. A free spirit, though he recognized that he would have to subjugate his private predilections to the social standards of the milieu in which he hoped to survive, he was never more than a recalcitrant spectator in these sophisticated snake pits. As we shall see, he diligently sang the praises of diverse heroes, but never of the milieu in which they gravitated.

Tristan's dislike for this courtly world was exacerbated by this gentleman's awareness of the failings of his class. Proud of his efforts to cultivate virtue as he was conscious of his many failings, he was particularly sensitive to the "degeneration" (a term he used, like Corneille, in its etymological sense) of his peers. He saw the merits of elevated birth—but only when accompanied by personal worth—a geneology adding luster to virtues, but not substituting for them (*La Lyre*, "Les Soins superflus"). The rampant self-serving scrambling of mediocrities was a constant source of sorrow to this sensitive person who, though a failure by all the standards of courtly life, knew himself to be superior to those who all too frequently succeeded.

What Tristan would have liked most, was to be able to enjoy the simple pleasures afforded by nature: the sounds of birds and of cascades, the sights and sounds of forests and meadows would have enthralled him all day long. Instead, he was forced to associate with people who had little use for such inclinations and amusements, preferring to become "slaves of men and of money" (*Les Amours*,

"Plainte à la belle banquière"). As I have already said, Tristan felt that only at court could he prosper as a poet. Happiness away from a person such as Gaston was not even conceivable, as he confessed to a future protector, the Duchesse de Chaulnes. This, in spite of the fact that he knew very well that the activities of courtly life were hardly conducive to poetic production: "Poetry prospers only in idleness; . . . as it is difficult to simultaneously embrace an active and a contemplative life, it is difficult to simultaneously be a great courtier and a great writer. . . . The Muses demand leisure, and court demands curtsies. Whoever gets up early to see lots of people, feigns to espouse many causes, and meddles in many intrigues, will never succeed in being a great poet" (Letter 88). A free spirit, he could only hope that the most discerning of the courtiers and princes would understand his wants and needs, and give him the opportunity to serve them by granting him the leisure and the freedom to develop his talents in their service.

This is the only possible explanation for the loyalty and the faithful manner in which he fulfilled the duties associated with those social functions which he could barely tolerate. These were the virtues of which he was justifiably proud. His attachment to the ungrateful Gaston d'Orléans, so touchingly elaborated and explained in a message to his brother (Letter 81), goes far beyond the call of duty, and seems reasonable only when viewed in the light of the aforementioned hope.

Tristan's most striking descriptions of court life, and his most bitingly ironic comments on it, are due to the frustration of that hope. For over twenty years, Tristan served Gaston, not for his pleasure, but for his glory, as he states in *La Lyre* ("A Son Altesse Royale, faisant l'état de sa maison"). Small wonder that he asked his master: "Will you unfeelingly see that my heart has served you for fifteen years in vain?" In another poem to this ungrateful master, he wonders how much longer the lamp which has shed light on Gaston's glorious deeds can burn without oil (*La Lyre*, "A Son Altesse Royale"). When Gaston obviously refused to respond, Tristan enlisted the aid of friends at the princely court. Eventually, a feeling of discouragement, of fatalistic weariness, crept into his poems. In several poems he follows the timid hope that somehow things are bound to improve with the notion that, if they do not, he can always go home and seek solace in the bosom of his beloved nature (*La Lyre*, "Les Divins suffrages," "Ode à Monsieur de Chaudebonne", etc.). In such poems, he asks his friends to cease their entreaties on his behalf, preferring to resign himself to his miserable state. In "Ode à Monsieur de Chaudebonne," he acknowledges that he will never be happy far from Gaston and his court—a desperate statement at best—but he also recognizes that he may have to give up the precarious position he holds there, hoping to find if not happiness, at least solace in the country, where "the gold of the sun, the silver of mountain brooks, the enamel of wild flowers will suffice, as will the gems of the stars when the silence and coolness of night encourage his dreams." Then, were some catastrophe to befall such a retreat, he would have the consolation of friends. But even such escapist dreams are tinged with bitterness: where is he to find such a retreat? "Where it is not a crime to love faithfulness; where sincerity is esteemed, . . . and where some prince, to his glory, will grant a pittance" to the poet.

When Voiture, a friend and colleague at Gaston's court, did him a favor, Tristan acknowledged it with a bittersweet poem, in which he states that servitude has crippled his most beautiful lines: "Can one with equity crown faithfulness with what one offers to artifice?" (*La Lyre*, "Sur un bon office reçu"). When this "ungrateful and avaricious century" continued to deny him the "honest leisure so necessary to good writing,"[1] he was forced by penury to appeal to precisely the type of courtier he most despised, those who through servility and chicanery had risen to favor; and it is these people he was forced to praise, hoping they would intercede on his behalf. Several such poems are already to be found in *La Lyre*. "Daphnis, fais-moi raison" speaks of twenty years of unrewarded service. Apollo had given him hope of immortality, but of what good is that? "If one is so poor during one's lifetime, what is the good of a great reputation after death?" "A Monsieur le Comte de Brion" unites the recipient and Gaston in basest flattery, as does "A Monsieur L'Abbé de La Rivière." In the latter poem, the recipient being a poet himself, Tristan asks him to grant the wishes of the Muses who recommend him, but the tone is far from bantering; it is obvious to even the most uninitiated reader that Tristan, ill and in dire need, is desperate.

It is in the *Vers héroïques*, however, that this plight and the resulting bitterness are most visible. In an ode to La Rivière, he points out that he is very good at his trade, and that he is ready to use this talent in the service not only of Gaston, but of Gaston's favorite, flattering both with hopes of immortality via his poetry. While this ode is relatively restrained and limited to base flattery, a set of *stances* to the same man is far more urgent: Tristan risked his life for Gaston who, though "good and generous," has obviously not done his duty and fulfilled his obligations toward the poet. Now, if the good abbé does not second his plea, the poet will have lost "both time and trouble" and all evidence favoring him will have been in vain. Showing the ode to another of Gaston's courtiers, he wrote, with growing bitterness, that "all the fruits of my labors have until now only been paid in coin of ungratefulness" ("A Monsieur de Patris"). There were limits to his ability to flatter—or his willingness to do so—and "A Monsieur Bourdon" shows him relegated to an attic chamber, in utter discomfort, because he could not bring himself to "flatter, spy, or betray," or generally to be endowed with what "this twisted century calls virtues."

By 1645, Tristan obviously had had enough of such a life, and he entered into the service of the Duchesse de Chaulnes. Gaston, whom he still considered "a divinity," had abandoned him. In the already quoted passage from "La Servitude," we have seen how proud he could be, refusing to beg at a door or a table for the bread that he deserves and which is not offered freely. In the rest of this long poem, he points out that since Gaston does not want him and will not keep him properly, he must serve this most charming mistress who will perhaps better recognize his "frankness and faith," because hers "is not a court where the importunate crowd of fortune hunters produces a thick shadow between himself and the light of day." He goes on to state his hope that his new patroness will fill his needs without his having to connive, intrigue, and be unfaithful to himself. He points out that he loves his freedom, but that the sacrifice thereof would be relative, for the woman to whom he sacrifices this freedom is endowed with such virtues that the loss pales before the gain. The poem thus ends on a note of jubilation and hope, although based on such a conceit that it is difficult to give it total credence.

The honeymoon was indeed of short duration, and Tristan seized the first opportunity to abandon the duchess. When she left Paris to establish her residence in the Auvergne, a rather desolate region not far from Tristan's Marche, he claimed ill health so as not to have to accompany her, and entered into the household of the Duc de Guise. In a set of *stances* addressed to his new master, he openly admitted that there was "nothing harsh in this servitude" that might afflict him. It can be safely assumed that much of Tristan's relative happiness was due to the fact that his patron was away most of the time, thus giving him both a pension and freedom. Even when home, the Duc de

Guise obviously expected Tristan to sing his praises and to speak of his amorous and martial accomplishments, but never to fawn and scheme.

Tristan's last years were, therefore, somewhat more secure than had been his earlier ones, but the relative good fortune came too late to entirely reshape his thinking toward court life. We do not know whether he wrote his own epitaph while still in the unsettled milieu of Gaston's court, but he did not deny it when it was published in 1648:

> Elevé dans la cour dès ma tendre jeunesse,
> J'abordai la Fortune et n'en eus jamais rien,
> Car j'aimais la Vertu, cette altière maîtresse
> Qui fait braver la peine et mépriser le bien.[2]

Far from modest, but eminently appropriate, this epitaph is amplified with bitterness in "Prosopopée d'un courtisan":

> Ebloui de l'éclat de la splendeur mondaine,
> Je me flattai toujours d'une espérance vaine,
> Faisant le chien couchant auprès d'un grand seigneur.
> Je me vis toujours pauvre et tâchai de paraître,
> Je vécus dans la peine attendant le bonheur,
> Et mourus sur un coffre en attendant mon maître.[3]

This vivid description of any courtier, fawning, poor, and unhappy while fortune and fame elude him, is painfully autobiographical.

II The Heroic Ethos

As J.-P. Chauveau has pointed out, certain *ancien régime* poets were fortunate enough to be protected by the crown, and their poems thus became apologies of the monarchy as a sacred institution. By choice, or by circumstantial necessity, Tristan was attached to what must be called "the opposition," and he thus became the bard of the aristocratic ethos with all the vestiges of feudal individualism and pride that were to lead to the Fronde and eventually die in the splendor of Versailles.[4]

The heroes to whom Tristan erects his verbal temples are, like those of antiquity, demigods, offspring of gods or, at least, of other demigods. Such is the basic premise of *La Renommée*[5] and of every heroic poem that precedes it. From the beginning—the word "temple" is Tristan's own—this pagan theology is superimposed on the Christian one. "A la Sérénissime Princesse Isabelle" is an early ode that lauds a devout ruler, enunciates all her Christian virtues, and then enshrines her in such a way as to "make the heavens jealous." Gaston is, of course, "first among our demigods" ("A Son Altesse Royale sur ses autres progrès en Flandre"), for while the station of these heroes may vary, they are always the poet's protectors or would-be protectors. Eventually, of course, de Guise takes Gaston's place, and is lauded as the "offspring of a hundred demigods" (*La Renommée*).

As is the case with so many worshippers (Mariolotry is no exception), there comes a time when the initial postulate—and its fundamental limitations—succomb to the fervor of the faithful. The demigods are, of course, "superhuman" (*Vers héroïques*, Sonnet 34), but they soon transcend their intermediate (and intermediary) status. Gaston, initially "another Achilles," is soon better than Achilles (*Ibid.*, "Sur la prise de Graveline"), and is even taken for Mars himself (*Ibid.*, "La Mer"), as is Vladislas of Poland (*Ibid.*, "Ode Royale"). It is therefore quite natural that the king himself be treated only with the greatest of hyperboles, and such is indeed the case in "Minerve au Roy" (*La Lyre*), a series of laudatory ejaculations such as the following:

> Ton âme n'aspire qu'au bien;
> Ton coeur abhorre le vice,
> Et ta valeur n'entreprend rien
> Qu'après avoir consulté ta Justice[6]

each one being followed by the reiterated question: "Is there a God more divine than you?"

The "esprit, grâce et courage" with which these heroes are endowed (*La Lyre*, "A M. le Grand. Ode") are, of course, inherited, but that is not enough. They must be assiduously cultivated, and only through such cultivation can the hero hope for a certain freedom of action and mastery over his own fate (*La Lyre*, dedicatory letter to M. de Montauron). Without this individual effort, heroes are bound to "degenerate," that is, to fail to live up to the expectations derived from their essence, thus to become slaves of fate.[7] Of course, the stars interfere even with the plans of the greatest (*Vers héroïques*,

"Eglogue maritime"), but if these use the presents of the Fates with wisdom and magnanimity, that interference is an equitable one. It is thanks to such equity and benevolence that the reign of Charles of England is a "golden age" (Ibid.), and it is thanks to this destiny that, despite envy and ignorance—the major foes of these heroic virtues (A L'Honneur de Monseigneur le Chancelier. Stances)[8]—the stars of these demigods cannot be dimmed by any earthly forces.

Even their glorious deaths are but a part of an assured apotheosis that forever enshrines their glory. In that sense, the numerous "tombeau" poems have the same purpose as those lauding the living: from the moment the gods grant the capability for greatness to the final apotheosis, every deed, every display of greatness, is a part of an eternal state for which neither chronology nor duration has any meaning, both being the mere realization of what both the poet (Vers héroïques, "Sur la prise de Graveline") and the Fates had predicted. The Fates and the gods lean over the hero's crib at birth. The poet sees in his genealogy and virtues the confirmation by the existence of the predetermined essence. In short, time is abolished since every act, even the last (glorious death leading to eternity), merely repeats or accentuates what was enshrined from the start. Each act is, therefore, an exemplar rather than a part of an historic chronology. If anything, it repeats and confirms the great deeds of the ancestors, thus restoring the hero to his destiny. These "instantanés," as Chauveau calls them, synopsize for posterity the entire significance of a life in which miracles are the norm. As he goes on to point out, such poems are, therefore, very akin to the official portraits of the time, which present the hero "in the most advantageous pose, at the precise moment at which his destiny is realized".[9]

If the poet dares to break in on this statuesque or pictorial isolation, it is only insofar as he associates himself with the entire tableau, as a medieval artist might have included himself in the background of his apocalyptic fresco. And such is his right, for the poetry, like the heroic deed, is imbued with a spark of the divine. In the preface to the Vers héroïques, Tristan refers to the "gods" to whom poetic incense is due, the verbal "statues" he is erecting to their glory (a glory that will last forever precisely because these "statues" cannot, like stone, be touched by time). In other words, he speaks of a "temple" in which both icon and priest are simultaneously of this earth and transcending this earth. The great stars of this earth eventually find their place in the Heavens, where their luster never dims (La Lyre, "Sur le trépas de Monsieur le Marquis de Coüalin"), but before that ultimate moment, the glory of the hero is dependent on the poet, whose task it is to make that glory manifest: Troy is gone,

> Et de ses Palais superbes,
> A peine les fondements
> Se trouvent parmi les herbes,[10]

but Homer lives on, and through him, Achilles and Hector (*Ibid.*, "A Monsieur de Montauron"). Tristan's poetry has only to find appreciative readers for the heroes he lauds to gain immortality.

Of this, Tristan was confident, though he knew that his public would always be restricted, one with "goût" and "discernement." Since he did not seek the approbation of all, but only that of an intellectual elite, his poetry, and his heroic poetry in particular, is highly intellectualized, rich in protracted metaphors and in the type of allusions that only the initiated or the learned could savor.[11]

The "statue" erected in this "temple" not only had to please the discerning worshipper, but, first and foremost, it had to please the idol, the patron or patroness. In a letter to the Marquis d'Aytone (*Lettres*, 2) prefacing the *recueil* honoring the late Infanta Isabella, he told his would-be protector how he had consulted the subject of the poem during her lifetime to assure that the portrait would be pleasing. The temple was, in effect, the result of a collaborative effort, since the Infanta had "instructed" the poet in order to "enrich" his work. The case, by no means unique, is particularly interesting because the poem in question, the "Ode to the Infanta," is one of the few heroic poems that is not a static portrait. Rather, it is a long biography which shows the evolution of the Princess to her position of virtue and glory, though even here there is something akin to a long fresco that depicts an entire history, if only to highlight the greatest episodes, the salient features which are concentrated in the present and its implications for the future. Multifaceted, the subject appears more human than that of the portraits. The poem is nevertheless one of extreme artifice, the past used as a gigantic backdrop to bring out the present, and the whole tensed in a barely contained leap to the future—a future which, ironically, was "frozen" by the untimely death of the Infanta.

Obviously, in such stately depictions, the foes, like the heroes, must be stylized and symbolic. Like the portraitists of his day, Tristan is—if I may be forgiven the anachronism—an incurable Romantic: the Milanese snake; the Belgian lion crushed by a modern Hercules; the sun shining on raised swords, and the glints in the eyes of his heroes which strike down the enemy or, at the very least, fill him with awe and terror; such are the graphic details that enrich the icons and statues filling the temples of the demigods.

There is perhaps no finer example of this type of poetry than "La Mer", an early poem first published in 1628 and reprinted with important variants in the *Vers héroïques*. It is basically a poem of nature, with superlative descriptive passages which I will discuss later on, but that nature is sandwiched between an opening reference to the death of a friend—and, obliquely, to Gaston's heroism at the Ile de Ré, the site of a military engagement in 1627—and a long coda (the last sixty lines of the poem) in praise of the victor. For all that, the poem is not as disjointed as some critics have claimed. It soon becomes apparent to the careful reader that most of the mythological references in the main part of the poem reappear in the last six stanzas, thus linking Neptune and his domain with a rival of that god, Gaston. Key metaphors, first introduced in the descriptive part, find their justification in this heroic coda. Thus a pirate, at first a seemingly gratuitous addition to the description of the sea, serves as a standard by which Gaston can be measured: the usually hardened pirate cannot master his fear of the storm, but Gason, according to all the prophets, will soon add the domain of Neptune to his own. By the same token, Gaston, "all in flame," like the rising sun, is first linked, then likened, to that symbolic entity of nature and its representative divinity. The prophets have foretold it (lines 195-96); he has already proven his divinity, and many more occasions to do so will present themselves. It is then that Tristan will truly sing his praise:

> Ce sera lors qu'avec des vers
> Qui naîtront d'une belle veine,
> Je ferai voir à l'univers
> Que ta valeur est plus qu'humaine:
> Mes traits auront tant de clartés,
> De pompe, d'art et de beautés,
> Que l'Envie en deviendra blême,
> Et baissant ses honteux regards,
> Pensera qu'Apollon lui-même
> Ait écrit les gestes de Mars.[12]

The storm at sea is obviously over; so is that which prevailed in the poet's heart (line 2). The future is assured, fame and glory await the princely god and the no less divine bard who will record his exploits. Gaston and Tristan, Mars and Apollo, integral parts of the nature described, yet both imbued with the creative genius that will allow them to shape their own destinies, both are immortalized in the "statues" that fill this poetic "temple."

CHAPTER 5

Poetry: Nature

I Images and Impressions

ALTHOUGH many seventeenth-century French poets professed
to love nature, only two before La Fontaine managed to
describe it with any degree of success, Saint-Amant and Tristan. For
both, nature is apt to be populated by mythological characters or
supernatural ones at times becoming phantasmagoric, but the description, nevertheless, can be vivid enough to convince the reader
that the creation is the result of personal observation and not merely
the repetition of commonplaces—though these abound both in
theme and form. If Tristan's descriptions seem at times to defy the
realistic bent one might expect of an observer of nature, it is because
this lover of nature is also a poet whose images and metaphors must
evolve along lines and follow dictates that are poetic rather than
materialistic. Furthermore, Tristan, like Saint-Amant, did not see
the role of the poet as that of a copyist. Therein lies both much of
his creative genius and of the source of misunderstanding that has
hovered over his descriptive poetry.

In the preface to his *Franciade*, Ronsard spoke of descriptive poetry
as being "a painting, or rather imitation of nature." Théophile de
Viau, in "La Maison de Silvie," also used the expression "traits
vivants d'une peinture"; but for Tristan, such is not the case.
Saint-Amant had described a perfect work of art as "surpassing
nature" ("Sur un portrait du roi"), and Tristan agreed, viewing
descriptive poetry not as a copy, but as an intellectual recreation on a
higher level, an idealized one to be enjoyed all the more because its
full appreciation depended on the mind as well as the senses. Nature,
under these circumstances, is a starting point, not a model to be
slavishly copied. Viewing the sea, Tristan exclaims: "Is this not one of
the beautiful objects ever formed by nature? Is this not one of the
beautiful subjects to be taken up by painting?" ("La Mer"). Nature

spreads its "tableau" before his eyes, and the artist can do no less when inspired by it:

> Flatté du doux bruit d'un ruisseau,
> D'un esprit plus clair et plus beau,
> Comme à l'enui de la peinture
> Qu'étale partout la Nature,
> J'entreprendrai votre tableau.[1] (*Amours*, "Promesse à Philis")

His art, like that of nature, is a creative process, a rival of nature's. *Ut pictura poesis*—a perfect tableau for highest enjoyment.

The relationship between poetry and the plastic arts cannot be overstated here, for there is an obvious cross pollination. Not only are many—if not most—of the paintings of Tristan's day of literary inspiration, but Tristan, like many of his contemporaries, was inspired by the techniques of the plastic arts. Whether he describes the man-made nature of a park or the wild countryside, Tristan always gives his tableau an architecture, a form. Even water is frozen into some form, and the sea of his famous ode is mineralized into "carved jasper." Visual evocations, his waves and ripples are frozen or crystallized, his expressions caught in mirrors or stone. This static quality, however, is most deceptive. Baroque countrysides, whether in print or on canvas, are imbued with an aura of disquiet. The first impression of bucolic serenity is ever spoiled or at least disturbed by a shivering sensation that all is not as it might be. In spite of the order, there is a hint of chaos; in spite of the apparent calm, there are signs of localized struggles that threaten to invade the entire land or seascape. These hints of struggle give a sense of drama, of activity. Motion may be frozen, but without losing a sense of imminent movement.[2]

Like these paintings, Tristan's landscapes can be divided into two broad categories. If the description is of a locus (*amoenus* or other), the space in question is enclosed. If, on the other hand, the scenery is merely the site of a reverie, or expected to suggest such, it will be one of vast, expansive vistas, functions of form I will dwell upon later in this chapter.

The first category is best represented by literary or mythological subjects, or by representations of specific places with no less specific references, public or semiprivate, e.g., Poussin's "Seasons," Lorrain's "Acis and Galatea," or Rubens's "Castle of Steen." What strikes the viewer at first glance is the enclosed, "framed" site, with a definite form and shape. No less striking, and of even greater interest

here, is the lack of uniformity in graphic details: trees, clouds, rock
formations, all lack detail and "realism," so that they are remarkable
only by certain specific traits made manifest by brilliant interplays of
light and darkness. Thus, the trees framing the castle of Steen,
though impossible to identify botanically, are the most striking
feature of that part of the canvas. Likewise, in Poussin's "Et in
Arcadia Ego," the massive trees are notable primarily for the source
of light that is hidden by one of them, and the rocks and branches of
"The Inspiration of Anacreon" are without reality, though imbued
with an aura that pervades the entire scene. Such a nature, particularly of the type depicted in Poussin's "Seasons," is imbued with a
mood. It is no longer a mere description, but it becomes the site of an
event, or the vehicle for a message. Small wonder that many of the
poetic descriptions of the time seem directly inspired by such
paintings.[3] The poetic landscapes that result are anything but photo-
graphic, though they do not lack linearity. Highlighting salient
features carefully selected to contribute to a central idea, they give,
rather than a "vue d'ensemble" in the graphic sense, a mood to be
shared; rather than visualizing "the" countryside as the poet did, the
reader is expected to associate it with one he knows, a process that
gives immediate life and relevance to the location.

The vast, expansive vistas that categorize the second type of
landscape are more conducive, both in painting and in poetry, to
reverie. Here again, the parallels are readily established. Claude-
Joseph Vernet's "Marine Sunset," with its subtle luminosity, or
Claude Lorrain's "Goatherd at Sunset," which seems to present a
proscenium of darkness from which the natural escape is the layered
luminescence of the distant landscape whose horizon is undistin-
guishable from the iridescent sky, are plastic counterparts to the
descriptive passages of Tristan's "La Mer." There, the interplay of
light and darkness at dusk is rendered by the description of night and
day simultaneously reflected on the same seascape, where the setting
sun is clouded in mist, shining through thick and dark clouds, and is
reflected, showing "mountains of shadow and sources of light."

In either case, the poem, like the painting, is a recreation,
presented less to make the reader rush out to see the country for
verification and enjoyment than to make him marvel before this new
masterpiece of creative art, one that strikes responsive chords in the
reader, that relies on his ability to unite memories of past perceptions
with the tableau presented by the poet. It asks the reader to

participate in the creative process by implanting in his mind less a total tableau than the key elements of a descriptive metaphor which the reader then superimposes on the canvas of past experiences or conceptions to thus obtain a new work of art inspired by the sensibility of the poet made effective by the cognitive power of the reader.

It might be objected that a poet deals with chronology while a painter deals with linearity, but the dichotomy was far from rigid in Tristan's time. Tristan, like his contemporaries, constantly tried to freeze a specific moment (such as dawn or dusk) while still suggesting life and movement, each frozen moment nevertheless giving hints of the immediate past and the imminent future. Painters likewise united the two concepts. Poussin's "Landscape with a Snake" depicts, in the foreground, a snake that has just killed a man. Another man sees the result and flees in horror while a woman, who has not seen the initial deed, is merely startled by the man's fright. Beyond all these, a still peaceful countryside is peopled by those going about their business, oblivious to the progressing drama. Here, then, a chronology is given linearity and dimension, with depiction of the drama in its early stages and graphic hints as to its consequent scenes, a reversion of the process that the poet must use to "describe" a countryside.

Of course, such a process is dependant on a great deal of artifice, however subtle its use might be properly disguised since art, like all expression of thought, had to appear "unstudied"—"plus elle est négligée et plus elle est charmante" being the catch phrase. Tristan always adds to his descriptions enough personal allusion to give an effect of naïveté, as when the beach at low tide reminds him of the "great plowed fields" of his native Marche ("La Mer"). But even that process is an intellectual and self-conscious one, the resulting lyricism being polished and controlled, not hermetic, but highly distilled, forcing an awareness of the semiotic value of the ingredients of description and of metaphors, of mythological and historic characters. Items that seem at first extraneous to the descriptive process reveal themselves to the careful reader as being far from gratuitous, contributing as they do to the semiotic value of this highlighted nature.[4] Because of these procedures and their implications, I cannot agree with those critics who emphasize either Tristan's predilection for still waters or rushing ones, depending on the critics' thesis, for Tristan uses water—as he uses all elements of nature—to make a point or to establish an ambiance and, as I hope to demonstrate later in this chapter, the characteristics of these elements are dictated by the goal of the poet.

For all this, it must be admitted that Tristan is not always as successful in all his descriptive attempts. Although he tries to appeal to all the senses, he cannot, for instance, evoke the olfactory sensations as well as did Saint-Amant. And while there is much musicality in Tristan's poetry, he is best when evoking or using soothing sounds. Nowhere in his many aquatic evocations do we get the admirable descriptions of thundering waves breaking on the shore, of a shuddering, boiling, foaming Nile, rising to heaven in wavy hills or swallowing itself in bottomless whirlpools, as Saint-Amant reveals to his readers in his "Moïse sauvé." The opening lines of the "Eglogue maritime" *(Vers héroïques)* do make the attempt, but are only partially successful, while in the second try (11. 81–84) the assailing waves of line 81 are quickly metamorphosed into liquid pearls.[5]

Therefore, it must be admitted that while Tristan speaks of both still and moving waters, he invariably mineralizes the latter. Whatever its struggle may be, with pebbles or shore, in light or in darkness, moving water is always described as jasper or glass, pearls or silver. The perpetual movement of the sea is frozen even as the sun tries to see its reflection in the rough waters:

> . . . les flots de vert émaillés
> Qui semblent des jaspes taillés,
> S'entre-dérobent son visage,
> Et par de petits tremblements
> Font voir au lieu de son image
> Mille pointes de diamants.
> . . . .
> Les vagues d'un cours diligent,
> A longs plis de verre et d'argent
> Se viennent rompre sur la rive,
> Où leur débris fait à tous coups
> Rejaillir une source vive
> De perles parmi les cailloux.[6] *(Vers héroïques,* "La Mer")

Though this sea fights with the sun, as fire does with water, whether during a period of relative calm as shown above or when winds, "to extinguish the celestial fires, carry water to the heavens," as bolts of lightning streak the black night, the most prolonged imagery is not that of light vs. darkness, but of the transformation of this most protean of elements into immutable gems, the ultimate metamorphosis which, by contagion, even crystallizes the sun's reflection. As in "Le Promenoir des deux amants," the moving waters struggling with the static rock yield to the nature they fight and, without ever ceasing to evoke motion, are frozen into the tableau.

II   *Habitat and Influence*

It is not infrequently said that the purpose of a painting is "to be." Such is not the case with the majority of the paintings used as points of reference in the first half of this chapter, for they, like the poems discussed, have a statement to make, explicitly or implicitly.[7] Tristan's land and seascapes are likewise meant to carry a message, or at least to prepare the reader for one.

In Tristan's religious poetry, it may be said that the painting is the message. Nature, created by God, is anthropomorphized so that it may adore God:

> Les fleurs à ce premier réveil
> Semblent s'éclore d'allégresse,
> Et se tourner vers le soleil
> Pour adorer Votre sagesse.
> Les petits oiseaux dans les bois
> Honorent en diverses voix
> L'Auteur de ces clartés naissantes.[8]
>
> (*Heures*, "Adoration et prière pour le matin.")

Such a nature's sole purpose is to prove, by its order, the existence of a benevolent and omnipotent God. It is safe to say that it is the exception, existing only—and rarely—in the religious manuals written or translated by Tristan.

With that notable exception, all of Tristan's nature is intended as a backdrop for something else, be it seduction, reverie, praise of a personage or beauty, or consolation. This is why such descriptions are so replete with mythological references—which act as hyphens between the locale and the message—and with prolonged metaphors—which tie the reality described to the human experience, be it intellectual or sensorial. This is why Tristan—like many of the so-called Baroque poets, especially those imitating Marino and his countrymen—chose to disregard the dicta of Malherbe concerning prolonged metaphors. In "Les Larmes de Saint Pierre,"

Malherbe had used a great number of long metaphors, but after 1600, he shunned them, and most of his contemporaries, poets and critics alike, agreed, calling their use a "vicious practice." Tristan readily saw that only through the use of prolonged metaphors kept up by a series of relays could the "painting" and its message be unified.

One of the best examples of prolonged metaphor, or rather of a system of closely connected metaphors, is "La Mer." At first glance, the poem seems to be a series of disconnected tableaus (the sea at dawn or at dusk, storm or calm, high or low tide; people at sea; Gaston's fortune), and so have most critics viewed it.[9] But in fact, these tableaus are all tied together by recurring images, structures, and allusions, the metaphoric continuity further enhanced by such seeming banalities as the recurring contrasts between light and dark, fire and water.

Maricour, a friend of Tristan, had just died in an engagement led by Gaston. The poem opens with a reference to this death and to the poet's grief, attenuated only by his contemplation of the sea. It ends with a prolonged praise of Gaston and his feats of arms. Between these two statements, there is a long description of a changing sea. But this ode is not "to" the sea; it is "to His Royal Highness" about the sea. The rising storm at sea is like the storm of grief in the heart of Tristan, and no less like the storm that rages within Gaston's breast. The poet and the unfortunate prince, like the storm-tossed pilot of the poem, may well feel despair, their "art and valor confounded" by the hostile elements—i.e., the Fates. But the reverie that has led us from the empty dejection or passive grief to the storm, now leads us through that storm to the calm—light and darkness interiorized like the storm itself. The entire seascape is thus viewed as a metaphor, with the sea being the forces of inner feelings that man must confront to purge himself and above which he must rise. Nature thus does more than console man: it forces him to find himself within himself. That part of the poem which praises Gaston is thus linked to the descriptive portion in several ways: he is contrasted to the pirate scared by the storm; he is also the god who defied the sea, rising out of it in full glory; furthermore, his fiery countenance is a reprise of the Apollonian metaphor prevalent in the early parts of the poem. And it is to his personification that Tristan finally allies himself as the bard of light and order. In other words, from the first line, the reader is presented with a series of relays that will make the transition from the descriptive stanzas to those concerned with human endeavors a natural and smooth one. From the outset, we are given references to the sea's power to "charm" with its protean magic; this will recur throughout, until the real magic, equal or superior to that of the divinities of the sea, is identified as emanating from Gaston. The beautiful description is thus seen to be a basis not only for establishing an aura of consolation, but also as proof of Gaston's divinity.

If "La Mer" is a good example of a description of a broad vista, "Le Promenoir des deux amants" is a perfect example of the *locus amoenus* to which the poet brings his lover. The poem opens with an appeal to all the senses, though the quiet tonalities do not so much awaken these senses as soothe them. The proper mood for the tryst having been established in the first five stanzas, Tristan switches to the theme of solitude, assuring his Climène that this is the perfect place to bring her: while in the first part he had described only the microcosm of the grotto and the "promenoir," in this second part he describes the surrounding mountains and forests that isolate and insulate.the propitious spot.

This ideal spot, properly filled with symbols of love that contribute to the reader's ability to recreate an erotic fantasy, is constantly contrasted—tacitly or explicitly—with the world of salons and of court, demonstrating the gulf that exists between society as it is and as Tristan would like to see it. More important, it reveals directly that this locus is more pleasant and more propitious to amatory endeavors than the one from which he lures Climène and from which he is himself escaping. Since this is basically a poem of seduction, direct address is prevalent, but used with deliberate ambiguity. Is it merely the beloved, or the reader as well, whom he is trying to lure to his deserted walkway? It might be argued that the poem is intended for her only, but the title speaks of the lovers as third persons, offering "the two lovers" as spectacle. The ambiguity is, therefore, intentional. The repeated demonstratives used to point out the pleasant features of this ideal location give them a sense of immediacy; they are right there before her (our) eyes, to be seen and appreciated, and in which she (we) is (are) to be immersed. The evocative power of words is here demonstrated at its best, the distance between the scene described and the lady brought to it being annihilated. Stressing the safety of the place, its isolation, quiet, and privacy, the poet creates a new reality—physical or psychological—which the lady will want to share. Here again, we are faced with the notion of a "paysage" as an "état d'âme": this *locus amoenus* is as much mental as it is physical, and it is in a psychological as well as sylvan labyrinth that Tristan wishes to lure Climène . . . or any given reader.

The actual description is, therefore, fairly limited and subservient to the creation of a mood, an aura of peace and privacy. All bespeaks of pristine, primitive conditions, unspoiled by man, full of harmony and primeval order. The meadows with their flowers are a bejeweled rug awaiting the lovers; the birds sing, but only because the mountains, the woods, and the stately trees protect them from hunters and other nefarious aspects of civilization; the brook once rushed, but now it is transformed into a still pond whose reflective surface seems to wait for the image of the lovers' faces, mirroring, meanwhile, the flowers and reeds of the shore. Thus, with commonplaces, Tristan establishes a perfect relationship between the locus and its visitors, and this— wherein lies his originality—largely by means of a series of tensions and relaxations of rhythms that echo the feelings he tries to evoke (for instance, the rise to a climax in stanzas 22 and 23, a tension he relaxes momentarily for a more dramatic rise to a new tension toward the finale).

Beyond this formal struggle, there lies a thematic one between the notion of idyllic tranquility and the latent disquiet in the poet himself, the lover who allows not only some ambiguous mythological powers to pass through the site, but also points to proof of the passage of previous lovers. References to benign struggles such as those between water and rock, light and darkness, two turtledoves, etc., all sound like subsurface counterpoints to the general aura of serenity. The pond itself is not without ambivalence. As G. Genette has put it, "Water is the locale of all treachery and of all inconstancy: in the reflection it offers him, Narcissus cannot recognize himself without misgivings, nor love himself without danger."[10] This gives rise to a strange ambiguity: one sees a reflection that is simultaneously oneself and another (as the rising sun is surprised to find "another sun" upon seeing its reflection in the water).

This duality is further compounded by a stillness-movement dichotomy. However still it might be, water is nevertheless disturbed by the slightest movement or breeze, and the beloved image can therefore be instantly destroyed—even by the person creating the image. In the case of running water, the problem is further compounded, since there may be a stable image on an unstable mirror. An added danger, as Genette points out, is that any surface suggests a depth: "The end which threatens a reflection on water, and which expresses its paradoxical existence, is death by engulfment."[11]

And yet, there is a logical explanation for all these disquieting elements in the poem. By presenting such benign signs of discord, the poet forestalls the arguments that his lady love might bring up. By making them so readily reconciled, he quiets her fears: the water relaxes, the birds stop their quarrels, Diana yields to Venus. Anthropomorphized, the elements of the nature surrounding the lovers all call upon them to love and to become one with nature. Here again, the originality of Tristan is demonstrated as the clichés of the feminine *blason* (cherry lips, rosy cheeks, zephyr-like breath) become "natural," while those of nature become anthropomorphized. As the lovers enter into the spirit of the locale—we are once again reminded that "le paysage est un état d'âme"—they become one with it, the figures of the painting melting into the countryside.

Although the *locus amoenus* is most frequently considered as a trysting spot, such need not be the case, and this "pleasant locale" is, for Tristan as for poets since antiquity, the ideal place in which to recover from the hardships of court life. In one of his earliest poems, "Ode à M. de Chaudebonne," probably written in 1625, after a brief trip to his native Marche, even the rugged countryside and the climate of home are described with longing and affection. Though the land is too poor for grapes, its hills are seasonally covered with the gold of rye and the enamel of flowered meadows. The limpid streams, the starry jewels of night, and the sapphire and ruby dawn are evoked to console him from courtly disasters: "The music of a thousand birds, the noise and fall of waters which rush from the rocks, and the shade at the height of the heat . . ."—these are the things that will compensate for his misfortunes.

This is the theme he takes up again and again. In "Plainte à la belle banquière," after a prolonged metaphoric trip on the sea of unrequited love, he recovers from his shipwreck, his ailing spirits will be cured by the perfume of flowers, cascading waters, "the sweet concert of birds," and the pleasant woods and meadows. There is no doubt that he overstates his case when he affirms that he loves only the simple pleasures of nature, of a life away from the deceit and bustle of court. It is a theme he uses most frequently when he despairs of getting support from a patron such as Gaston d'Orléans; but he no less often admits that there can be no happiness away from this court and culture. The threat or lure of a pastoral retreat—a commonplace in itself—is one which is only wistfully called upon for poetic expression, never one to be taken too literally. It is while stretched out on the grass, under a tree, that he may best dream and "paint" the portrait of Philis (*Amours*, "Promesse à Philis"). In moments of great sorrow, such as at the death of his friend Maricour,

he may "abhor the noise of court and love only solitude" ("La Mer").
He may say that it is only in the countryside that one tastes the
"purest pleasures of life" (*Amarillis*, 5–12). I, nevertheless, get the
impression that, for Tristan, trees are the confidants of forlorn lovers
(*Panthée*, 341–46), and nature is the "safe asylum for those mistreated
by fortune" (*La Lyre*, "Plainte de l'illustre pasteur"); but it is not a
desirable permanent habitat.

When human contact is painful, when a political or erotic adven-
ture has gone awry, and when even friends cannot be entrusted with
confidences, then the "inhabitable deserts" become the "sweet
walking places of the unfortunate" (*Amours*, "Pour les yeux de*"). On
such occasions, the most rugged of natural settings, "the deepest
woods . . . most solitary deserts . . . rocks whose drop is so steep and
rough" seem sweet and hospitable to him (*Lettres*, 78). This is not
meant to imply that nature responds to the unfortunate poet; rather,
that on such occasion, he wishes to pour out his heart to an insensate
entity (*Plaintes*, "Chanson"), for it is nature's mere proximity and
contact that lead him to introspection (*Amours*, "Plainte à la belle
banquière"). As a result, neither night nor the darkness of the forest's
densest canopy is of itself negative or terrifying; both add to the
impenetrability of the aforementioned "safe asylum." The woods as
asylum and consolation of the unfortunate lover was a theme as old as
antiquity and as new as Guarini's *Pastor fido*, but Tristan was able to
give it a new value by means of the elegiacal tones that pervade such
poems (as when, in "L'Orphée," Orpheus charms nature with his
music, a cliché revitalized by the musicality of Tristan's verses).

Of course, there are moments when nature becomes unwelcome.
Generally consoling and soothing in a passive way, it continues its
own life without intervening in that of the poet. As a result, it may
become importunate, as when a radiant springtime countryside
provides too stark and painful a contrast to the poet's morose mood.
When the poet, while on a dangerous mission, is traversing a
countryside foreign to him, it is easy for the normally enchanting
features of nature to suddenly take on frightening aspects:

> Le soleil se va perdant;
> La splendeur dont il éclate
> Peint là bas dans l'Occident
> Un grand fleuve d'écarlate.[12] (*Vers héroïques*, "Terreurs nocturnes.")

The problem is that this scarlet river takes on, in the poet's vivid and already oversensitized imagination, all sorts of frightening attributes and becomes the source of a terrifying phantasmagoria.

These are rare exceptions and, in spite of their excellence, they should not obscure the fact that, in general, Tristan's nature is impassive but soothing (a role already prevalent, as I have said, from antiquity to Tristan's time, and which was to become a commonplace during the Romantic period). This nature, by its steadfastness, invites the poet to confide in it, to find in it echoes of his innermost feelings, to transcend petty travails, be they social or erotic, and, by allowing him to pour out his heart, to discover himself within himself, thus finding peace.

CHAPTER 6

Poetry:The Heavens

I *Tristan's Stars*

IT is in the bosom of Mother Nature that Tristan most frequently views the stars; and his stellar poetry is generally a soothing one, though the heavens can frighten, as in "Terreurs nocturnes," where they are part of a phantasmagorical world. They tend, at times, as in the religious poetry, to be the ordered proof of divine creation. The starry night is, most frequently, a blanket of security in which the poet wraps himself, a source of well-being and of peace that permeates him and his poetry:

> Douce et paisible nuit, déité secourable,
>   Dont l'empire est si favorable
> A ceux qui sont lassés des longs travaux du jour,
> Chacun dort maintenant sous tes humides voiles,
> Mais malgré tes pavots, les épines d'amour
> M'obligent de veiller avecque tes étoiles.[1] (*Plaintes*, "L'amant discret.")

This is the same "cold, damp night, inciting to rest" of the "Plaintes d'Acante," the titular poem of the collection, the "cool, somber and solitary night, repository of secrets . . . and mother of rest" of "La Servitude," which gives solace to even the most tormented of lovers.

While the firmament as a whole may be reassuring, Tristan views the individual stars in a totally different light. Independent of divine will, the stars are imbued with a force and a will all their own: "Clear ornaments of heaven, asters, brilliant causes which give order to all things . . ." (*Vers héroïques*, "Prosopopée de la fontaine de *"). Their mysterious influence seems gratuitous and fickle to the poet, who addresses them as others would God. He knows quite well that they neither respond nor care, that rebellious ejaculations are wasted, and that a fatalistic submission is the only wise course of action: "My days

64

will come out of their night," says he in the famous "Ode à M. de Chaudebonne"; things are bound to get better, and if not, so be it. Only on rare occasions does he believe that the stars can be fought. In "A M. le Comte de Brion" *(La Lyre)*, he enunciates the belief that, if enough great souls unite to fight his evil star, he may yet prevail; but such optimism is rare indeed. These stars, then, are deaf to our pleas in this vale of tears: "The laws of destiny do not correspond to our desires," and our years are filled with "infirmities, troubles and calamities," with more problems than the lowliest animals and few advantages over them *(La Lyre,* "Les Misères humaines").

Everything—good or bad—that has ever happened to him is due to the stars under which he was born *(Le Page disgracié,* ch. 2). Even in love, his stars are hostile: "The all-powerful stars, which are hostile to me, will not relent" ("Plaintes d'Acante"). If, in love, passion destroys all reason, that too is the result of the stars' influence: "An all-powerful destiny, an invincible star, attach a somber veil over my reason's eyes" *(Panthée,* 327–28). Not even kings are immune from such a fatality; and when a king succumbs, as in *La Folie du sage,* he can only recognize the justice of his defeat: since the lady-love deserves his total subjugation, by "accepting her rule," he "follows his destiny" (247–50). This is not a dramatic device restricted to Tristan's plays. He says no less in his lyrical poetry:

> Je ne sais quel astre invincible
> A qui tout effet est possible,
> M'a versé d'un secret poison,
> . . . .
> . . . et défend à mes sens d'écouter ma raison.[2] *(La Lyre,*
>   "Plainte de l'illustre pasteur.")

At times—and such is the case in this particular poem—the star in question is "a sun," but not the one above: the obsessive metaphor is present even in the amorous "Plaintes." The sun that illuminates his darkest shadows is the woman he loves and whom he then describes in a most sensuous stanza, which introduces her metamorphosis into sun—and the no less startling metamorphosis of the "plainte" into paean:

> Je vois sa taille ravissante,
> J'apperçois sa gorge éclatante,
> Sur qui flottent ses beaux cheveux,

> Ces précieux filets, et ces tresses fatales,
> Qui pour les libertés font de nouveaux Dédales,
> Et qui serrent les coeurs d'indissolubles noeuds.[3] *(Ibid.)*

Burning in the nets of her radiant hair, he goes on to wish that a real fire—surely a lesser one—had come down from heaven to consume him.[4] Of course, by a clever conceit, the stars can also be the eyes of the beloved, as dazzling and domineering—and as destructive of initiative and rationality—as the stars in heaven (*Panthée*, 359–61). Before such a dazzling display, the poet can only acknowledge them as "my kings, my stars, my destiny" ("Le Promenoir des deux amants").

It would be wrong to liken the poems in which Tristan complains of the stars' nefarious influence to the excessive lamentations of some of his contemporaries. The restraint, the aristocratic modesty that pervades all of his work, reduces the plaints to melancholic musings. As he said to Chaudebonne, who wanted to help him when he was in need: "Let destiny run its course; if the heavens wish to persecute me, so be it; they will either relent or I will seek solace in the countryside." Unlike Théophile, Tristan was too much the gentleman to howl from the rooftops, and, to a crushing fate, he would only oppose a fatalistic melancholy, a restraint and "pudeur" not unlike that demonstrated in his erotic poems.

II   *The Fate of Heroes*

As I have stated in an earlier chapter, fate decrees at birth what the life of a highborn person is to be. The hero who does "degenerate" is, therefore, fated to realize his essence by his existence, his every act; by following in the footsteps of his ancestors he is doomed to play a game of theme and variations: he may improve, but he cannot innovate. In short, such a hero can only reincarnate the greatness that his ancestors put in him. Such is always the case when Tristan sings the praises of victors and fortunate Maecenas, and such would always be the case if all of Tristan's patrons and would-be patrons had been fortunate in all of their endeavors, felicitously tripping through the turbulent middle of the century. Unfortunately, that was not so.

We are, therefore, confronted with a rather thorny problem. On the one hand, we have great personages of history whom fate allows to fulfill the expectations of their birth. On the other hand, we have equally meritorious people persecuted by a jealous fate, one that, far from just, decrees that the greater the merit of the victim, the more he is "worthy" of the persecution (*La Lyre*, "Consolation à Madame la Princesse Marie"). For such people, "the brilliant causes which give order to all things and at times trouble the conditions of demigods" are blind to innocence in their seemingly capricious influence (*Vers héroïques*, "Prosopopée de la fontaine de *"). The answer derived from a careful reading of Tristan's work is relatively simple: the stars that preside over one's birth may have no feelings; the Parcae they unleash have feelings indeed. The stars may "shower roses around the cradle" of Cinq-Mars (*A Monsieur Le Grand. Ode*), they are unrelenting in their enmity towards Gaston d'Orléans, who must constantly struggle against them to make his valor manifest (*Vers héroïques*, "A Son Altesse Royale, sur ses autres progrès en Flandre"). In either case, the stars act without the slightest consideration for the people involved, never responding to pleas, never guided by human considerations or values. They are kind to Cinq-Mars—at least in Tristan's ode—and inimical to Gaston upon whom they unleash envious Fortune without the slightest consideration for earthly justice. The stars do not respond to human demands, but they do interfere in human activities, however indirect such interference may be. Dame Fortune can be very fickle at times: "Fortune is more reasonable today; Heaven changed the season which was so dark and offensive toward your destiny" (*Vers héroïques*, "A Son Altesse Royale sur la prise de Graveline").

Instrument of the stars, fate—or the Fates—is generally evil, envious of virtue and beauty:

> Le sort dont la rigueur contraire aux belles choses
> Ternit si tôt les roses,
> Pour les plus beaux objets a le plus de courroux.[5] (*La Lyre*,
> "Consolation à la Princesse Marie.")

This is because fate is jealous, "its hatred always centered on virtue," the worthiness of a person determining the extent to which the attacks are "deserved." The cliché of the ephemeral rose reappears with fair frequency in Tristan's work, usually linked with a comment about fate's cruel unfairness, as in this consolation:

> Le sort tyran des belles choses
> Ne laisse durer qu'un moment
> Le vif éclat des roses.[6] (*La Lyre*, "Consolation à son cher ami.")

Carpe diem is the only logical advice that can come from such a finding, and he advises his friend to live for the moment, forgetting the dead, a theme taken up again and again, as in *La Lyre*'s "Consolation à Madame *** sur la mort de son mari" and in "Consolation à Idalie" from *Les Plaintes d'Acante:*

> Le temps qui sans repos va d'un pas si léger,
> Emporte avecque lui toutes les belles choses:
> C'est pour nous avertir de le bien ménager,
> Et faire des bouquets en la saison des roses.[7]

Such "consolations," relying as they do on a rather airy cliché, are a far cry from the more somberly stoic tone that Tristan used with equal frequency, as in the beautifully Horatian—and Malherbian—consolation to the Comte de Mons that appeared in both *Les Plaintes* and *La Lyre:*

> . . . dans les malheurs qu'on ne peut éviter
> C'est accroître son mal que de s'en tourmenter;
> Cette ordonnance passe encor qu'on en murmure.
> Et par la fermeté d'un courage constant,
> Lorsqu'on ne peut gauchir la mauvaise aventure,
>   On la brave en la supportant.[8] ("A M. le Comte de Mons.")

Generally speaking, the consolatory poems of Tristan are neither glib nor stoic, exuding rather a strong aura of Epicureanism reinforced by his stress of friendship and cerebral pleasures. Insisting on the notion that virtue is the source of all well-being, that ataraxia is preferable to intense pleasures, he rejects the fear of death as proper for either sufferer or spectator. To him, however, there is none of the Christian's joy at being reunited with God—even Sénèque, in *La Mort de Sénèque,* is more motivated by his search for peace and tranquility than by a desire to see his new-found God—but rather in evidence is an Epicurean rejection of the fear of death itself. Ariste's praise of death (*La Folie du sage,* 173–84), and Mariane's escape from her tyrannical husband via a death she does not fear (*La Mariane*) are, as we shall see, the dramatic counterparts of a poetic theme that pervades much of Tristan's work.[9]

This "état d'âme," coupled with his strong sense of decorum and propriety—allied, of course, with his peerless poetic talent—have given us some of the best consolatory poems of the century. "Sur le trépas de la Sérénissime Princesse Isabelle," reprinted in *La Lyre,* but aptly called "Peinture du trépas . . ." in the original edition, is indeed a painting, a stately tableau of a country in mourning, but one whose words emit the pompous music of a funeral march as muted and decorous as the noble subject demands:

> Par une loi fatale, autant comme elle est dure,
> Et dont aucun mortel ne se peut affranchir,
> Notre grande Isabelle est dans la sépulture,
> Et les cieux entr'ouverts viennent de s'enrichir
> Du plus rare trésor qui fût en la nature.[10]

As all the cities of Flanders come to pay homage, their heralds surround the body lying in state to form a most striking tableau:

> La Flandre la vint voir portant cent belles villes,
> Peintes sur un manteau de fin pourpre de Tyr . . .

but neither these "hundred beautiful cities," represented on this fine mantle, nor the respect due her royal blood, not even her "great virtues" could preserve her "from the rigor of the Parcae." In a mixture of pagan and Christian elements so typical of the day, Tristan reminds the reader that the fates have little regard for Christian virtues and even less for regal standing, harking back once again to Horace's *"Aequo pulsat pede,"* "death strikes with an indiscriminating foot."

III   *God*

Much ink has been spilled over whether Tristan was a libertine, a good Catholic, or alternatingly both. With carefully selected snippets, it is easy to prove anything. We have already seen that some of his poems are imbued with Epicurean ideas; others with Stoicism; still others with a most orthodox Catholicism. Tristan was obviously very eclectic, very knowledgeable, and—at least in his earlier years—anything but deeply committed to a particular credo or way of life.

There is no doubt that, in his youth, Tristan frequented many milieus in which libertines thrived. The court of Gaston was favorable to both types of *libertinage*, i.e., of mores and of ideas. It is therefore logical to assume that Tristan, an avid reader, readily came under the influence of freethinkers such as Vanini, Bruno, and the Neo-Epicureans such as Gassendi.[11] But while traces of these influences can be

found in some of his poems, there are just as many citations possible
that prove the opposite. I tend to agree with Amédée Carriat,[12] that
Tristan was probably inclined to libertinism in his youth, and that he
was not scared off by Vanini's death or Théophile's disgrace, since he
wrote to the poet afterwards and even made his friendship public in
one of his letters (71). It may be that he was temporarily exiled from
Paris in the mid-twenties—resulting in the "Ode à M. de
Chaudebonne"—because of that friendship. On the other hand, I
agree no less with Catherine Grisé, when she says that "although his
friend, Théophile de Viau, was a well known libertine and deist,
Tristan's works show no evidence of such tendencies." Like Grisé, I
believe that Tristan "seems to have been an intellectually and
artistically independent man who belonged to no particular
coterie."[13] Cyrano, another freethinker, had the highest praise for
Tristan: "He is the only poet, the only philospher, the only free man
that you have."[14] But that merely proves that one great mind admired
another, not that they shared the same ideas. As I have already
stated, Tristan was proud of his probity, his freedom, and his
faithfulness in friendship; he was also a great poet and knew it; Cyrano
agreed and appreciated him. It proves nothing else, least of all that
they travelled under the same theologic umbrella.

Many of his letters and dedicatory poems were written to friends
whose libertinism is beyond doubt, but too much has been made of
these. The letters either show an intellectual neutrality—though
accompanied by vehement professions of loyalty and friendship—or
orthodoxy, as is the case of letters 81 or 84. The liminary poems,
written to help friends sell their wares, are not as revealing as some
committed critics would have us believe. Dassoucy's *Ovide en belle
humeur* and Scarron's *Virgile travesti* are funny and irreverential, but
hardly earthshaking in their libertinism, and the lines that Tristan
wrote for them are nothing more than friendly bantering praise that
never goes beyond a then fashionable intellectual stance. It must be
remembered that it was dangerous to publish truly libertine poems.
That may explain his reticence. But that same reticence proves
nothing.[15] Though Tristan acknowledged having a reputation of
being "more libertine than bigot" (Letter 84), he never went beyond
that acknowledgment, and gave no food to the rumor.

In 1633, he included a poem entitled "Amour divin" in the
Plaintes. Five years later, he toned down the title to "La Sage
considération" for inclusion in his *Amours*. In 1639, he appended a
very pious sonnet to the first edition of *Panthée*, "A Jésus-Christ, dans

une maladie," in which he betrays greater worry over his soul than over his body. In a second poem appended to the same play, "Tombeau de feu Messire François de Bridieu," he praises the piety of the departed and rejoices at his sure entry into heaven. If the first poem has some sparks of sincerity, the second does not; like the "Amour divin," it is a collection of pious commonplaces rendered in poetic clichés. Certainly Amédée Carriat is right when he states that there are no signs of religion before that, and few between that and the publication of the religious manuals.[16] As Tristan admitted, "the best days" of his life were steeped in "long errors" (*Office*, "La Pénitence"). In these religious manuals he incessantly bemoans the waste of his youth in sinful endeavors; and one cannot attribute all these outpourings of faith to convention and façade. Like Carriat, I see in these signs of a somewhat belated but entirely sincere conversion. According to J. Loret, a gazetteer of the time, Tristan deserved to go straight to heaven, his piety "being known and commented upon everywhere."[17] I believe that a look at the poetry of the manuals will convince the reader that this was no façade.

Be it due to the religious revival that followed the initiation of the Counter Reformation, or, more specifically, to Louis XIII's consecration of his kingdom to the Virgin, a veritable vogue of devotional manuals was in evidence when Tristan published his *Office* in 1646. These guides to religious expression and meditation, mixtures of prose and poetry, French and Latin, stressed the dependence of any religious experience on introspection.

Possibly the most striking aspect of the religious revival which took place in France, and indeed throughout much of Europe, at the end of the sixteenth century and the beginning of the seventeenth century, was the lay movement towards a more personalized commitment to the Christian life. It seemed that the most logical way to intensify one's spiritual life was to imitate the devotional practices of those who dedicated their whole lives to prayer in the monastic life. So, numerous prayer books, manuals of meditation, treatises on the progressive stages of prayer, translations of the Roman Breviary and of the Little office of the Blessed Virgin Mary were published as aids to piety for the laity.[18]

These manuals, regardless of their titles, were "spiritual exercises" of introspection, contrition, and rededication.

It is, therefore, no surprise that the poems of the *Office* and of the *Heures*, no less than those of the *Exercices spirituels* can be seen to follow the example set by such spiritual guides as St. Ignatius de

Loyola and St. François de Sales. In his *Spiritual Exercises,* Loyola used a pattern of first setting the theme on a visual background, so that the penitant could contemplate it; then, he would present the comparison of the speaker / reader to previous sinners; and, lastly, he would set forth a colloquy (with Christ or the Virgin) of prayer and contrition. One of the best of Tristan's many adaptations of this scheme is "*La Pénitence.*" He opens with a vivid visual presentation: "Lord I call unto you from this solitary place. . . . I cast myself against this earth from which you drew me." As the foulness of his sins overwhelm him, the terseness reinforces the basic meaning: "In this tear-bathed humility, . . . I am so horrified and ashamed that I cannot speak." In the stanzas of this second part, the six quick beats of each last line are masterpieces of effective understatement. There follows the consideration of self and the ensuing self-abasement before God, the key sentiments, as in all the stanzas, being stated in the first and last lines: "I respected your Holy Majesty too seldom . . . and I break your Law." Tristan then opens the colloquy announced in the first line of the poem, asking for undeserved mercy in a stanza of remarkably balanced contrasts:

> Faites que votre Esprit dans mon coeur prenne place;
> Que sa divine ardeur vienne fondre la glace
>   D'un si grand endurcissement;
> Et bien que mes péchés vous demandent justice,
>   Ne souffrez pas que je périsse
>   Dans cet aveuglement.[19]

The Salian devotional exercise, though perhaps less rigorously structured, also follows a definite pattern frequently adopted by Tristan: first comes an "examen" of oneself, then a prayer either of thanks for a righteous day or of remorse for a sinful one.[20] Tristan's "Prière pour le soir après l'examen" (*Office*), to use but one example, proceeds by means of a series of questions that the faithful must ask himself: "How did I apply my senses to the honor of your service? By what innocent sentiments did I turn from vice? How . . . ?" Once these questions have been posed and answered, the good Christian sees the extent of his failings and can pray accordingly.

Whatever the intention of the genre might have been, it had its dictates and exigencies. Introspection does not mean mystical experience, but analysis of one's personal relationship with God; nor does it imply the individual's freedom to interpret: the intolerance of the

Counter Reformation demanded not creative worship, but adher-
ence to dogma and custom. Tristan could thus not be expected to
innovate in content, but in form only; indeed, he often managed to
give to the poetry in question the stamp of his creative genius. Many
of his religious stanzas add the richness of Baroque imagery to the
biblical metaphors:

> Des méchants j'ai suivi la troupe;
>   Buvant dans une même coupe,
> Je me suis enivré du vin des voluptés;
> Et l'habitude prise en ce désordre extrême,
> M'a réduit à tel point que l'iniquité même
> Devient le châtiment de mes iniquités.[21] (*Office*, "Prière
>   à la Sainte Vierge pour obtenir de son
>   Fils notre Sauveur la rémission de nos péchés.")

Though I have spoken of "a" genre, one is not to think of a unified or
monofaceted output. The manuals contain every conceivable form of
poetry conveying a variety of moods and ideas. To my mind, nothing
in the *Exercices* comes close in poetic achievement to the best of the
Heures and *Office*, such as "De Profundis," but on the other hand, the
excessive artifice that mars some of the earlier poems—such as the
puns of the "Stabat Mater"—is also gone, and many of the translations
of the *Exercices* are models of mood creations. "Pour le Carême," a
translation of "Audi benigne conditor," begins gently, never aban-
doning the even, plaintive mode that leads to the final supplication.
The first stanza is typical, the four line sentence forcing the reader
into a low pitch recitation whose basic tone is reinforced by the muted
sounds that predominate:

> Dans ce jeûne sacré sous qui nos corps gémissent
>   Durant quarante jours,
> Doux sauveur, dont jamais les graces ne tarissent,
> Oyez nos humbles voeux, soyez notre secours.[22]

We have here an example of classical simplicity devoid of unnecessary ornamentation. "Pour le jour de Pâques" heralds Easter with all
the pomp of a royal event:

> Sortis des rouges flots, vainqueurs de la tempête,
> Parés de vêtements où brille la blancheur,[23]

the glory of the Savior will be sung in appropriate regalia and with no less appropriate tones.

Such is not always the case in the earlier manuals. "A Saint Laurent" is spoiled by excessive Marinism as the saint who died in fiery martyrdom is called a "Phoenix among saints, celestial salamander," whose "constance and faith are purified like gold in the fire that reduces [him] to ashes." Equally inappropriate, though sanctioned by usage, was the frequent infiltration in the poems of the *Office* of classical mythology: Minos is one of the more visible denizens of hell, and even a "Méditation sur le memento homo" brings in references to Paris and Hercules.[24] A third element found only in the earlier production might be called a carryover from salon poetry. In the opening lines of "Prière à Jésus Christ," Christ, wishing to die for mankind, regards the thorns and nails as "carnations and roses." This intrusion of the clichés of erotic poetry is particularly frequent in the longer poems, though it also appears in some of the quatrains dashed off to accompany the beautiful engravings. These flaws are deleted in the *Exercices*, but so are the vivid images and powerful metaphors that give life to the poems of the *Office* and the *Heures*.

Some of the most striking metaphors occur in the prayers heralding morning, in which Christ is the sun and the Virgin dawn—though in a few cases the latter representation is too imbued with the attributes of the divinity from pagan mythology—and all of nature adores the Creator in a joyful chorus of sound and burst of movement and color that rouses the poet (and the faithful) out of bed to open his heart and mouth to sing God's praises ("Adoration et prière pour le matin").

The strongest images and metaphors occur in the more meditative poems, particularly those associated with the passion of Christ and with the evening "exercise." Though some of the shorter poems are banal commentaries on the illustrations, many are lively, ejaculatory, short prayers, the "inner transports" advocated by St. François which, because of their brevity, can be inserted into almost every daily activity, "as the pilgrim might refresh himself with a draught of wine without breaking his journey".[25]

Many of the poems centering on the passion belong to the morning cycle, and in these an inherent sense of redemption counters the suffering of Christ. Since man's guilt has fashioned the chains and thorns of the Savior, there can be no elation. Rather, the "minister of these sorrows" ("Jésus pris et lié") is saddened and awed by the magnitude of his crime and of Christ's goodness. As the faithful one asks to be redeemed by the one he has enchained, the antithesis is partially resolved in a gentle happiness from which the sadness cannot be entirely washed away:

> En faveur de mon âme oubliez votre prise;
> Rompez tous ses liens pour la mettre en franchise,
> Et veuillez délivrer qui vous a captivé.[26]

The ties that bind Christ are also those that enslave the penitent's soul whose freedom depends on the mercy of Christ, which, to be operative, must overlook the transgressions that have caused the passion. The beautifully intertwined antitheses reflect the *dissidium* in the heart of the sinner: the serene beauty of Christ shines through the horror and the infamy of the crucifixion, but the latter forbids selfish elation. It is as though not even the joy of "et resurexit" could eradicate the sorrow of "stabat mater."[27]

Following the Loyolan tradition, many of these meditations, particularly those of the evening, are reflections on mortality. *Memento homo* and *memento mori,* calls to the consideration of the fragility of human life, of the cadaver subject to decay and the ravages of worms, are among the most powerful in Tristan's theologic arsenal. "In reading the evening cycle of meditations, one is struck first by the spectacular physicality of the death-bed scenes, of the leprous sores of the penitent, of the worms in the tomb . . . and one is constantly reminded of the concrete violence of the Old Testament, the smell of flesh and decay, the intimacy of corruption."[28] It is in the depiction of this horror and in the presentation of these travails of body and soul that Tristan excels. His "Méditation sur le memento homo" presents what Grisé has called "a dance of death," in which all are caught up to fall under the homicidal scythe of Death.[29]

No less successful than certain of these original meditations are Tristan's translations and paraphrases of some of the psalms. Ejaculations are best when spontaneous, but in longer poems, such spontaneity could lead to dangerous theological blunders. Much of the religious production of Tristan—and of his contemporaries—lies, therefore, in the realm of translation and paraphrase, the originality of the poet demonstrated by technique rather than by thematic innovation. As we shall see, it is with the *amplificatio* and *interpretatio* of biblical texts that Tristan gives us some of his best work in the genre.

"De Profundis" is a technical masterpiece. Each stanza is composed of three alexandrines, a prolonged cry for mercy, followed by a

brief but strong statement of hope, the shift in thought going hand in
hand with that in form:

> Du gouffre des ennuis dont mon âme est remplie,
> Et du milieu des maux dont je me sens presser,
> Ma voix s'adresse à toi, mon Dieu je te supplie
> De vouloir l'exaucer.[30]

To the rather bare call of the opening lines of Psalm 130, Tristan has
added a personal touch which he accentuates until the end, when his
appeal suddenly and most effectively shifts to encompass all of
mankind. The last short line is then a call for universal illumination,
the redemption of Israel of the Psalm transmuted into general and
eternal salvation.

One of the best examples of Tristan's skill in this realm is his
"Miserere," a lengthy and massive adaptation of Psalm 50. It is
replete with clever yet judiciously used metaphors, antitheses and
oxymora consecrated by biblical and patristic writings; yet these do
not convey a feeling of artificiality or artifice. On the contrary, they
contribute to an overwhelming impression of dedication, of peace,
and of harmony. The strongest antitheses do not betray inner
struggles, but surprisingly logical truths:

> Je méritais la mort et vous m'avez fait grâce,
> J'étais digne de haine et vous m'avez aimé.[31]

As in David's psalm, there is a perfect balance throughout between
contrition and hope, but Tristan expands and systematizes the
process, dividing each sestet into two units with three balanced lines
in each. To each hemistich he gives a value countered by the
following:

> Seigneur, j'ai mon recours, abîmé dans les crimes,
> A vos hautes bontés à ces profonds abîmes
> Qui sont toujours plus grands que notre iniquité:

When the need arises, as it does in this first stanza, he steps up the
pace, and the antithetical construction abandons the hemistichal
pattern:

> Encor que mes péchés méritent le supplice,
> Au lieu de me punir selon votre justice,

> Veuillez me pardonner selon votre bonté.[32]

No less skillful is the amplification. In the original, verse three merely reads "For I know my transgressions, and my sin is ever before me." Tristan changes this to:

> Je reconnais ma faute; une sourde tristesse,
> Qui me pique à toute heure et me ronge sans cesse,
> Est un bourreau secret qui me comble d'effroi;
> Mon coeur incessamment en reçoit quelque atteinte.
> L'horreur de mes forfaits me tient toujours en crainte,
> Et toujours mon péché s'élève contre moi.[33]

Here, the added dimension is one of duration, which amplifies the sense of constant torture and misery. To the matter of fact terseness of verses 11–12, Tristan adds a new momentum:

> Détournez de vos yeux l'objet de mes offenses;
> Mettez comme en oubli les désobéissances
> Dont mon ingratitude émeut votre courroux.
> Remplissez mon esprit d'une grâce nouvelle
> Et même dans mon sein créez un coeur fidèle,
> Mais un coeur qui vous aime et qui soit tout à vous.[34]

The major innovation here is a gradual and inexorable progression from the negative and despondent to the optimistic, one that parallels in miniature the structure of the entire poem.

It is apparent then, that, while most of Tristan's religious poems fall short of his usual standard of quality—and it may be surmised that Tristan sold his pen for pecuniary considerations—there are notable exceptions. Penury has nothing to do with sincerity, a sentiment that pervades the better poems such as the "Miserere." To fill the pages of a manual, Tristan had to produce a given number of poems, and some of these do seem like the work of a hack; to satisfy himself, he penned some of his best lines for inclusion, poems that are well-crafted and deeply moving. There is some sifting to be done here, but great benefits can be derived.

CHAPTER 7

Tragedy

I *Tristan and Classical Tragedy*

FRENCH literary critics have marveled in recent years at the fact that Tristan L'Hermite's theater has received more attention abroad than in his native country. And yet, this should not be so surprising. Not too long ago, speaking of French Classical tragedy, I said:

Tragedy, for Racine and Corneille as for Shakespeare and Webster, is an investigation of the human heart and mind in search of the limits of the human being. Why then is there so much confusion when French and American or English dramaphiles speak of their respective dramatists? . . . Shakespeare and Racine belong to two different social orders. Neither one is, of necessity, better or worse, but they are different. All one needs to appreciate either is not to insist on preconceived notions, or more precisely, one should not insist on reading the one with values acquired from the other.[1]

An oversimplification, perhaps, but one which is even more applicable to the question of the relative neglect of Tristan's theater in France.

Corneille and Racine, whatever their differences, were very much attuned to and in sympathy with the new social order, one which was moving toward order, decorum, civility, and sophistication, one in which there was little room for the Romantic—or, as I suggested in an earlier chapter, feudal—idea of a self-centered artist or hero. There are some vestiges of the feudal ideal in Corneille; there are none in Racine—and this may be why some of the last great feudal lords such as Saint-Evremond were so reluctant to join the camp of the Racinophiles. The French have rightfully enshrined these two great dramatists; but in so doing, they have set them up as standards by which all other writers are to be judged. Furthermore, they have extrapolated from their drama rules which are the essence of these

78

works, but which were never meant as universal guidelines. Tristan, as I have already said, was a "maverick," a man and an artist who, by artistic taste, personal ideals, and social ideas did not belong to—and could not enter—the new order. Two early rehabilitators of Tristan, in trying to bring him out of oblivion, presented him as a "Precursor of Racine,"[2] a comparison that could not serve Tristan well. Denying him an identity of his own, these two critics saw in him something he was not—an unfinished Racine—and failed to hear the specific timbre and tonality of Tristanian tragedy.

Tragedy, it must be remembered, was born in Greece at a time when the age of myth was yielding to the age of reason. It was reborn in Europe at the moment of the crumbling of what might be called the Thomistic edifice with its safe credo; or, to use the famous title of Paul Hazard, it was reborn at a moment of *Crisis in European Conscious-ness*.[3] Tragedy is indeed a literature of transition, of crisis, of mental awakening. The "mythologic" thought that earlier prevailed, moves in a cosmos of divine order in which man would like to participate. In that world, man's image of himself is derived from whatever his comprehension of the myth might be. Only a most precarious stability can be expected from such an ontology, and this was readily demonstrated when the age of discovery dawned, shaking the foundations of the scientific edifice sanctioned by Church dogma. Once man found his myth lacking, he had to seek answers elsewhere, and, like the Greeks of Aristotle's times, the French of Montaigne's and Descartes's times had to seek that locus within themselves, a frightening experience for any thinking person. It is this age of anxiety that is reflected in the tragedies of Tristan—as it is in those of Shakespeare.

Tristan is by no means "Shakespearean"; nor is he Cornelian or Racinian. Too French to have much in common with the Bard of Avon, he is too immersed in a period and mood on which Corneille turned his back, and which Racine only dimly recognized, to be fruitfully compared to either of these two giants. In theater, as in poetry, Tristan the artist, no less than Tristan the man, is a stranger. As we shall see, his plays are populated with reflections of himself, noble souls out of tune with their milieus—strangers.[4]

II *The Strangers*

The tragic hero is, almost by definition, an idealist—whether his ideal be one of goodness or of evil—lost in a practical world of relative values. Such a radical conflict is obviously insoluble, and the only suspense possible is not centered on "what," but on "how," for it is only in his rejection of facile contingencies and compromises—the "evil" he must overcome to be heroic and tragic—that the hero can achieve greatness, i.e., find himself and become himself.

The wrong sacrifices, the wrong choices predicated on false values, these are the evils visited on tragic protagonists, evils which these must reject by rejecting the world of base values. Racine's heroes who see this, in their profound humanity are loath to act on their vision, and much suffering precedes the final decision. Of course, it is these initial travails that elicit our sympathy, which becomes superfluous at the moment of transcendence. Thus Phèdre, who at the very beginning of Racine's great play, declares that she has come to bid the sun a final farewell, does not make her decision irrevocable until the last scene, and in *Bérénice*, an analogous separation is not made manifest until the end, when Antiochus's "Alas!" shows how far above the world is the tragic universe of Titus and Bérénice.

Racine's heroes reject the world, but not its basic values. That is precisely what makes their farewells so long and agonizing. Tristan's protagonists, on the contrary, reject the world because they cannot abide its values. Thus, destiny, imposed, but not accepted, may well crush a mortal, it cannot triumph over his will. It is only too easy, in such cases, to think of Pascal's *Pensée* 347: at the fatal moment, the hero is triumphant because he knows why he dies, but the executioner does not, or, as in the case of Camus's *The Stranger*, thinks of false reasons.[5]

These heroes are unable—or unwilling—to communicate with their fellow human beings. It is the resulting isolation which is the basis of their tragic situation. These rebels, with concentrated introspection, seek to establish their own identities, to find answers within themselves to basic ontological questions, hoping to derive therefrom viable or at least acceptable *modi operandi*. In short, a Tristanian protagonist seeks an authentic and dynamic *moi* in a basically unauthentic and static world, a situation that can only lead to a nauseous and noxious anxiety. The greatness of Tristan's heroes lies in their total lucidity: fully aware of the worldly absurdity, they refuse the balms of unconsciousness no less than those of compromise.[6] Like Corneille's Suréna, Tristan's protagonists die because they willfully choose not to live a lie. In that sense, they are active contributors to their destiny, succumbing because of their intransigence, proud witnesses of their foes' inferiority and, in the final analysis, victors over them, since these foes must witness in turn the enshrinement of their victims' superiority.

III   La Mariane

La Mariane was performed at the Théâtre du Marais during the Spring of 1636, a period of relative calm for Tristan, since Gaston d'Orléans was in temporary retirement in Blois. A landmark in the transition of French theater from the stiff, rhetorical, and declamatory pieces of the late Renaissance to what is now known as the Classical period, it had an instant and lasting success which not even the appearance of Corneille's *Le Cid*, some months later, was able to overshadow. Some have credited Montdory, creator of the role of Hérode, for the unusual crowds that flocked to the play. To be sure, the man who was struck down by apoplexy while playing the demanding role in August, 1637, had much to do with the initial success, but it is possible to make too much of this. There were ten editions of the play during Tristan's lifetime. Molière's troupe performed it thirty-four times between 1659 and 1680, and fourteen more times from 1680 to 1684, according to the register of La Grange. The register of the Comédie Française shows that it was performed thirty-eight times between 1680 and 1703. In short, the play maintained a more than honorable spot in the repertoire long after Montdory's personal contribution had ceased to be a factor. Furthermore, the play's popularity was international, witness the many translations throughout the seventeenth and eighteenth centuries. A true psychological drama, it contains some of the best lines in French drama, and certainly the best before Corneille's *Le Cid*. It is perhaps too declamatory for modern tastes, but it adds to Mairet's *Sophonisbe*, usually considered the first Classical play, a lyrical value theretofore unknown in the genre.

The story of Herod and Mariamne is well known, the version by Josephus (*De Bello Judaico*, I, 31) being the most famous. Suffice it here to give the broad outlines of this historic drama: Herod, of base birth, has crushed the power of the Hasmonaean dynasty and become ruler of Judea. To solidify his position on the throne, he marries Mariamne, a princess of the royal family, who bears him several children. Because Herod had killed her father and her brother, her feelings turn to hatred. Summoned by his Roman superiors to Rhodes, Herod leaves orders that Mariamne be killed should he not return. When she discovers this, Mariamne voices her hatred. When this is reported in exaggerated terms to Herod upon his return, he has her executed.

Tristan readily understood what his dramatic predecessors such as Luigi Dolce and Alexandre Hardy had not: that the broad fresco of history, with a large cast of characters and a plethora of psychological entanglements would not yield a cohesive and effective drama. He also saw that the basic idea—that of two people misunderstanding each other, with others fostering that misunderstanding—could give rise to an intensely dramatic nucleus. He therefore centered our attention on two characters, or rather on the wall rising between them. French critics weaned on less declamatory plays than those favored by a pre-Cornelian public, often find the play static. There is some truth to this, but this is a poem of solitude, of estrangement. That is its limitation; it is also its beauty, one to be fully enjoyed, not compared to something it is not trying to be.

As the play opens, Hérode is already the murderer of the last of the Hasmonaeans, Aristobule, the brother of Mariane. Mariane has also discovered Hérode's order for her death prior to his departure, a gesture dictated by ferocious jealousy, but which she simply views as proof of his lack of love for her. It not only condemns him in her eyes, but forces her to see her past gestures of love as aberrations beneath her royal dignity. Her outbursts of hatred and scorn will be gleefully reported and embroidered upon by Hérode's siblings, who deeply resent the princess' condescending ways. In view of this *a priori* situation, we are, as of the first scene, already near the crisis, the confrontation. On the one hand, we have a parvenu tyrant, conscience-stricken and full of doubts, yet one whose bravado and choleric outbursts frequently give him the upper hand; on the other, an unforgiving and unyielding princess who can forget neither the deeds of her husband nor his base origins.

The "argument" of the first act, as stated in the first edition, is ample demonstration of this psychological orientation (the numbers refer to the scenes of the act):

1. Hérode awakens with a start, troubled by a terrifying vision. 2. His brother and sister try to calm him by telling him of the vanity of dreams. 3. Hérode withdraws unto himself, recalls the friendship of the Romans and his own merits. 4. Having dissipated this fear, he complains of his love for Mariane by whom he would like to be more loved. 5. Phérore and Salome try in vain to speak ill of her. 6. Hérode sends for her, with the intention of obliging her to show more affection for him.

In this introductory act, Hérode declares his need for a physically absent, yet psychologically omnipresent Mariane. The second act, not surprisingly, will reverse the situation, and we quickly realize that Hérode and Mariane cannot live without each other. The tragedy resides precisely in that Mariane, failing to see that Hérode is as necessary to her hatred as she is to his love, rejects all his overtures and makes all communication impossible.

It would be wrong to see in Mariane a monofaceted and monomaniacal creature bent on the destruction of her husband and of herself. She once loved Hérode, saved his crown and his life (286);[7] and bore him children. His bloody deeds, and the misunderstood order for the possible death of his wife have changed her love into a blind and desperate hatred. She sees in him only "an abominable monster who appears to me covered with the blood of my relatives" (348–49). This is more than a figure of speech: night and day, the specters of the murdered Hasmonaeans appear before her (383–84); how can she love such a man? She would rather die (427–28). She realizes that she is Hérode's wife, but this cannot be allowed to infringe on her integrity or her memories of dynastic grandeur: "If my body is captive, my soul is not. . . . Let Hérode importune me with love or hatred, I will always live and die as a queen" (362–68). This royal essence, and her awareness of it, is as much responsible for the conjugal rift as any sentimental consideration, for she sees in Hérode a base commoner who, by his every deed, reveals that he cannot transcend his lowly birth, being motivated by petty desires, hampered by ignoble thoughts, totally incapable of self-abnegation or even of comprehending someone not likewise mired in pettiness.

Mariane's rejection of Hérode, and of any mention of his love, is eminently logical, yet does not quite ring true. She neither can nor wants to believe in a love that infringes upon a solitude so essential to her posture. But that posture is premature in the early acts of the play: she mistakes her moral superiority for a limitless self-sufficiency which exists only in her mind, for her hatred, essential to her identity, cannot exist in a vacuum. She incessantly goads him, and, as late as the third act, continues to taunt him with her moral superiority: "I suffer betrayals, but do not commit them" (814), she tells Hérode, reminding him of "a thousand betrayals, and a thousand cruelties, the murder of an ancestor, the assassination of a brother" (818–19), until Hérode's mounting rage makes him blurt out words of hatred—a sentiment he does not have, but one she understands, believes in, needs, and therefore, welcomes (857–58). Only then does she feel fully vindicated and free: "Believe whatever you say, and whatever you think," she tells her impotent interlocutor (980) as she decides to be a stranger at her own trial, foreshadowing Corneille's Suréna who, in an analogous situation, will tell his eventual murderer, "I will take care of my glory, you decide about my life." Hérode, by his outburst, at this lower level legitimizes the rejection dictated by Mariane's higher vision of things. Only then, when at peace with herself, can she truly cut all earthly ties and become genuinely self-sufficient—as Hérode becomes increasingly aware of his dependence on her—so that even the pity lavished on her by her mother and the soldiers leading her to her death is superfluous (1315, 1359–60). When her mother, afraid for her own life, loudly disowns Mariane (1379–90), the latter, understanding and without anger, simply replies, "You will live innocent and I will die guilty" (1392). The severance is complete; she no longer needs anyone or anything, not even the "shouts of hatred" sought by Camus's Meursault.

Even then, Mariane is more than an arrogant, self-destructive creature. Rather, she is an eminently moral being in an amoral, Machiavellian world. To find inner peace, she opts for values in which she can believe and which will make any externally imposed verdict meaningless. By her decision, she forces Hérode into an impasse from which he can exit only by murdering the unbearable witness to his debasement.[8] Her course of action is predicated on an easy choice: morality or gratuitous prostitution. Hérode's is much harder, being a shameful surrender to contingencies, relative values, even self-indulgence. It enshrines his impotence and dependence. Before the arrival on the scene of Mariane, to whom he owes everything (286), he was nothing; without her, he goes mad.

If, facing this proud and noble princess there were given only the "lamentations" and the effusions of a "monstrous, disordered, ever reiterated passion,"[9] there would be little dramatic conflict and less interest. Such is obviously not the case, and Hérode is, dramatically at least, Mariane's equal. Mariane resents Hérode's base origins and her own subservience to such a man. He, in turn, is rather proud of the fact that he has risen by his own devices to his position of power. He recognizes his debt to Mariane, and understands her pride, though he resents it. As he tells his siblings, "It is only fair, to tell the truth, that she maintain a certain majesty before you. A thousand glorious kings are her ancestors, and she can be called the daughter of our masters" (293–96). If he resents her taunts, it is less because they remind him of his genetic or moral inferiority than because, like any person proud of an ascending career, he cannot accept a derogation to his sense of independence and of accomplishment. Chafing under the distant yet subtly present yoke of Rome, he cannot help but lash back at Mariane whenever she points out his limitations.

By today's standards, Hérode is a monster; viewed historically, he is not. "Scepters belong to those who can seize them," says a character in *Dynamis* by Du Ryer, a contemporary of Tristan, and this seventeenth-century view was in perfect accord with that of antiquity. By the same token, Mariane's brother being very popular (412, 417–18), he had to pose a danger to Hérode, and again, viewing things in their historic context and perspective, "if it is granted that the safe-guarding of his crown must be a king's first concern, the murder of Aristobule, for example, was an inescapable consequence of the young prince's popularity."[10] Hérode should thus feel quite at ease; yet he does not. This may be ascribed to conscience, but that is an oversimplification in itself. Whenever he feels unsure about anything, he asks his siblings; but he senses that they have the same limitations of birth as does he. He wishes he could rely, as he once could, on the superior presence of mind of Mariane—a superiority he simultaneously welcomes and resents—but the woman who once cared for him obviously no longer does and can no longer be trusted. He would like to judge himself by his standards, but cannot do so while Mariane judges him by hers. Likewise, when he wishes to judge her, he has but to look at her to see that she is judging him (715–54); in each confrontation, Hérode the judge is transformed into Hérode the judged, and the inquisitor-turned-victim naturally lashes out at his tormentor with a savagery born of frustration.

Exacerbating Hérode's problem is the fact that he is very much in love, however warped and selfish that love may be by our standards (for it is a savage, possessive one). Whenever Mariane falters—as when she thinks of her soon-to-be-orphaned children—he mistakes her hesitation for a rekindling of love that gives hope to his own. Inevitably, "the King yields to the lover" (894), and it is as lover that he utters the ironically lucid line, "See how my fate hinges on yours" (905). Still more ironic is the fact that such outbursts can only make Mariane suspicious and strengthen her resolve to resist all his advances.

Thus, in the presence of Mariane, Hérode will falter at first; but in reaction to her resolute stance or outraged accusations, he will inevitably act to shut those eyes whose accusing *regard* he can not stand. Once the victim is removed, of course, once the judging eyes are no longer piercing him, he again falls prey to doubt: "How can I cause the death of one I have so loved?" (1244). He wavers, sensing that his mind is badly shaken (1247). Even after he has given the fateful order, he remains torn, alternating between hope and lucidity and, eventually, between sanity and madness. Though he knows that she is now dead, he interrupts his mourning to command that she be led back to him, apprised of his forgiveness. Too late, he realizes that he cannot live without her and, voicing his remorse, thinks of joining her in death (1798–1800). Even as he faints in the arms of his servants, he remains unaware that death has not only freed Mariane and forever separated them, but that it has enshrined her glory and his defeat.

Hérode loves Mariane and cannot understand her hatred; he is ready to forgive her for what he believes to be an attempt on his life, but cannot overlook his belief in her infidelity, and it is this alleged crime that leads to her execution. Regicide or adultery, both crimes exist only in the mind of Hérode; and they do so because Mariane has made all communication between them impossible. Mariane maintains her lucidity, thereby transcending her earthly problems; Hérode gains a partial vision of truth only to go mad.[11]

IV   Panthée

Tristan's second play was first performed either at the end of 1637 or the beginning of 1638. Though it managed to remain in the repertoire some twenty-five years, it had only a mild success, both in print and on the stage. Part of the failure has been ascribed to the fact that Tristan wrote the play specifically for Montdory who, as we know, was incapacitated before the play could be staged. It is true that *Panthée*, like *La Mariane*, has some marvelous, passionate tirades, and it is quite likely that Montdory would have done them justice and given the play a certain success. The unfortunate truth, however, is that *Panthée*, though great poetry, is only a mediocre drama, and deserves the oblivion to which it has been relegated.

The plot, like that of *La Mariane*, is rather simple: Cirus, after a victory, has captured Panthée, wife of Abradate, and entrusted her to his friend Araspe who, sure of his control over his feelings, knows that he will not succomb to feminine wiles. He nevertheless falls in love, declares himself, and, when rejected, threatens to use force. Panthée complains to Cirus, who graciously protects her, while Araspe pretends to flee. Sensing that she has caused a severe loss to her kind captor, and grateful to him for his generous behavior, Panthée, when reunited with her husband, convinces him to join forces with Cirus. Abradate is killed in the first battle and Panthée stabs herself to death on his body. Araspe, in despair, also commits suicide.

In the initial handling of the story (by Xenophon), and in several subsequent ones (by Hardy, for instance), the emphasis had been on the reluctant betrayal of a cause by a husband desperately in love with a misguided woman, and on the consequences of that betrayal. Tristan, in the employ of Gaston d'Orléans, could not use that emphasis, since his master was frequently taking up arms against his royal brother for diverse personal reasons. He therefore reduced in importance the roles of the two political figures, Cirus and Abradate, the former rather monofaceted and the latter episodic, and centered our attention on Araspe and Panthée, or rather on the passion of the first for the chaste princess. An interesting political story was thus transformed into a drama of unhappy love.

While this explains the basic structure, it does not explain its flaws. Tristan has taken two episodes from Xenophon's *Cyropedia*, but failed to weld them together satisfactorily. When Cirus—a somewhat ironic Salomon—settles the matter of Araspe's threatened rape, and Araspe disappears, the matter seems closed and the play appears headed for a premature conclusion, perhaps with the anticlimactic reunion of Panthée and Abradate. In the second episode, during most of which Araspe is out of sight and out of mind,[12] Panthée becomes the central figure and the focus changes radically.

That is not the only flaw. Basically, the entire situation is rather untheatrical: three main characters, each with his or her own main theme, each functioning on a plane in such a way as to forbid involvement with the problems of the others. Under the circumstances, they can only take turns expounding, without ever clashing or exchanging ideas. The results are frequent passages of great poetic beauty, but no drama of any consequence.

Considering that Tristan's patron was a leader of a rather disloyal opposition, the first public of *Panthée* must have been particularly sensitive to the apology of divine monarchy as expounded by Cirus, sentiments to be expected in writers such as Corneille, but hardly associated with the court of Gaston. Cirus makes it clear from the start that he considers himself an instrument of divine will. His lines ring with pompous music. A king must always

> Gouverner son esprit ainsi que ses sujets,
> Et mêlant la justice à des bontés extrêmes,
> En commandant autrui, se commander soi-même.[13] (190–92)

The majesty of these perfectly structured alexandrines is a proper reflection of the man and the aura that surrounds him. When Araspe violates his trust, the "crime" is considered by Cirus to be less against Panthée than against the reputation, esteem, and greatness of the king (883–86). When Panthée excuses Araspe, saying that his recent illness has perhaps shaken his mind (1010–11), Cirus is relieved, not because Panthée's wrath has subsided, but because his own honor is no longer involved if Araspe's lapse is "excusable." Likewise, the death of Abradate is viewed by Cirus with a monarchic eye; he wonders if he has been too kind to the foe in the past (1487–88), and readily clings to the first rationalization that comes to mind: Abradate will survive in his memory and in a thousand marble monuments erected in his honor (1497–1500). In lines of appropriate resonances, the king who is part of history thus promises to enshrine his new friend. Such is the image he transmits unrelentingly, and though the tragic news of the double suicide cannot fail to shake him, that will take place off stage after the final curtain.[14]

Panthée marvels at the good treatment she receives from a monarch who, were he to emulate his contemporaries, would enslave her or make her his concubine. She fails to understand that Cirus does not act out of kindness or devotion—his constant irony is ample proof of that—but out of generosity (the word being used here in its etymological sense). To his birth, to his station, to his concept of self, Cirus owes the impeccable and totally admirable behavior of which his treatment of Panthée is but a single instance. Cirus is a singleminded monarch aware of the obligations of his station. He views people and events only as pieces of his elaborate pedestal. He does not enter into the frame of mind of others, as they fail to penetrate his. He is a magnificent monument, uttering lines of solemn beauty; and these lines, like the man himself, are gems standing in relief without any connection to a coherent whole.

Panthée, as I have already stated, is totally foreign to the world of Cirus, and the music of her lines is a reflection of that difference.

Thinking only of her husband and of her love for him, she pours out her heart to everyone, whether they care or not. Like Cirus, she is less involved in dialogue than prone to deliver interrupted monologues whose dramatic impact is negligible but with undeniable lyrical qualities. "O Dieu! si tu savais ce que c'est que d'aimer" (435),[15] she exclaims to a maid of honor who can only assent. When she describes the man she loves, even the nature in which she sets him is imbued with life and beauty, but it is for the enthusiastic cataloguing of his features that words literally tumble forth, breathlessly:

> . . . j'ai cru voir sa taille et ses yeux et son teint;
> Le vrai ton de sa voix a frappé mon oreille,
> Son visage était gai, sa bouche était vermeille;
> Du bien de me revoir il rendait grâce aux Dieux,
> Et son contentement se lisait dans ses yeux.[16] (472–76)

When her husband is dead, her sorrow is as poignant as her joy had been contagious:

> Ton visage changé n'a point changé mon âme,
> Tu n'es plus rien que glace et je suis toute en flamme:
> Mon coeur est tout ouvert des coups qui t'ont blessé,
> Bien que tu sois parti, je ne t'ai point laissé,
> Mon esprit suit toujours ton ombre qui s'envole,
> Et ma bouche mourante à la tienne se colle.[17] (1593–98)

In a world whose motto is "Nil solidum," at least her love remains constant.

In contrast to these lyrical outpourings, Araspe's declarations seem *précieux* to modern ears. It may well be that Montdory could have delivered them in such a way as to move a sentimental public, but today they merely sound stilted and excessive. Coming so rapidly upon his forcefully reiterated statements that love can always be ruled by will, his declarations are imbued with a certain inappropriate comicality. Enhancing this unfortunate sensation is the fact that he is particularly prone to voice these sentiments at the most inopportune moments. Panthée has just finished relating to her maid of honor a dream in which she saw her husband first happily reunited with her, then dead and mutilated, when she happens to come upon Araspe who, oblivious to her mood or to her protestations, pours out his heart. Although he is, on occasion, sufficiently lucid to note that

Panthée loves her husband, and is thus simultaneously—and legitimately—"both his wife and his lover" (406), Araspe considers himself more often than not Abradate's rival, and never quite realizes that there is no place for him in Panthée's world. He is simply unable to face facts, and during his lyrical outbursts completely loses contact with reality. His glee upon learning that his "rival" is dead, shows that he is the last to understand that the death of Abradate is not the beginning, but the end of all hope for him. Panthée, faithful to her love, will follow Abradate in death, shutting Araspe out forever. If his final gesture—his suicide—proves his love, it changes nothing: whereas the world of the living, ruled by "Nil solidum," might have held some hope for him, the static world of the dead does not.

Lack of communication, as we have seen in *La Mariane*, can be a source of tragedy. Here, with parallel monologues by two deaf people, it is a source, if not of laughter, at least of mild and uneasy amusement. Like marionettes, these two lovers are so wrapped up in their own feelings and rhetoric that they cannot listen, understand, or communicate.[18] As a result, the first "episode" turns into an absurd melodrama of errors which Cirus unravels—with equal disregard for all those involved.

With Araspe off stage during most of the fourth act, one might have hoped for an improved dramatic texture. Such is not the case. The act lacks cohesiveness as Tristan tries to adjust the action of the play to a considerable set of events. Rushed, the defection of Abradate is badly prepared and shows the hero as a henpecked man of minimal moral fiber. When the fifth act opens with Araspe rejoicing at the death of Abradate, Tristan has managed to kill any sympathy a sensitive public could have had for either protagonist, and only Cirus's grandeur and Panthée's sorrow partially redeem the aura of solemnity expected of a tragedy.

In short, *Panthée* fails because it is a badly structured play in which characters obsessed with single passions give voice to feelings without listening to others, or even noticing whether they themselves are heard and understood. Tristan lavished some of his most beautiful lines on these characters. In or out of context, they are eminently worth reading, but they will probably never be heard from a stage again—and deservedly so.

V   La Mort de Sénèque

Late in 1643, or early in 1644, Tristan had his third play performed by Molière's troupe, the Illustre Théâtre. Three editions in as many years show that the play enjoyed an immediate success, due perhaps in part to the sterling performance of Madeleine Béjart in the role of Epicaris. After 1647, however, there were no more editions and very few performances, and the play soon fell into total oblivion. The reasons, as we shall see, are numerous, but unlike *Panthée, La Mort de Sénèque* is a powerful drama that deserves attention, not only from the student of literature, but from the lover of good drama; aspects of the play that caused its failure in the late seventeenth century need not bother us today.

The rather involved plot is drawn from the *Annals* of Tacitus, though several more modern sources were obviously also consulted. The excesses of Néron have led to a conspiracy against his life, headed by Pison. Epicaris, a freedwoman, tries to gain Procule to the conspiracy, but the latter betrays the plot to Néron. Epicaris is jailed, and the conspirators decide to rush through with their plot; but once again they are betrayed. This time, Néron seizes two of them who, under torture, implicate all of their cohorts and, in addition, Sénèque, who is innocent, having refused to join the group. Sénèque is ordered to kill himself. Fearing the worst for his wife, he grants her permission to kill herself and then goes stoically to his death.

One of the problems with such a plot is that it demands a relatively large cast and great mobility if verisimilitude is to be preserved. A few years earlier (as late as the première of *La Mariane*) this would have been no problem, but by 1644, compartmentalized stages were no longer in vogue, and to abide by the then solidly entrenched unity of place, Tristan had the entire story occur in a garden near the imperial palace, a far from perfect solution: the ease with which every character happens to come into that garden to discuss his or her innermost secret verges on the comic. With modern staging, such a problem would, of course, disappear without doing the least violence to the play or to the author's intentions.

The main reasons for the play's eventual failure lie elsewhere, though here again, the elements involved were considered unacceptable by a public whose tastes were evolving towards the famous "Classical" standards of Racine, but these need not be so judged by a modern public. Many critics have called *La Mort de Sénèque* Tristan's "most Shakespearean play," several of them undoubtedly considering this a derogatory judgment. They are, of course, quite right—whatever their intentions—and this goes a long way towards explaining the play's demise in France; but it is more a categorization than an analysis and need not stop us from appreciating the play for what it is.

In 1643, the age of Louis XIII came to an end, and, while the Fronde was just over the horizon, France was nevertheless in a mood for law and order, reason and rationality. The tragic stage, along with the pulpit, became a prime instrument for the propagation of this new credo, and tragedy was therefore expected to be decorous, proper, and unsullied by earthy or comic contacts. The world of Nero, on the other hand, was one in which values had been reversed and where decorum was either trampled underfoot or used as a thin and easily cracked facial veneer. It was, to use the modern idiom, a world of the absurd, in which the grotesque invaded all realms of human endeavor. Tristan's genius resides precisely in that he was able to capture this mood, to translate it into an artistic coherence, and to put it on stage. The earthy duels of wits between Sabine and Epicaris, or the teeth-grinding laughter that is evoked at the most horrendous moments, are but contributors to a general feeling of disorientation, of loss, and, eventually, of fear, that first grips the characters of the play to eventually engulf the reader or the viewer. Such a manic hell, from which there is no escape but death, had never before been experienced on the French stage. Tristan was to refine the process for his last play, *Osman;* it was Racine who perfected it and adapted it to the new exigencies in plays such as *Britannicus* and *Bajazet.*

La Mort de Sénèque deals less with individuals than with factions, each one of which has both active and passive members. The active "movers" are, of course, the most dramatic, but their more passive counterparts are not mere pawns. Conscious of the moves they are urged to make, and of the potential of such moves, they are the real loci of tragic action; and, though critics have spilled much ink over Epicaris and Sabine, Néron is no less interesting, and Tristan was right to give the title role to Sénèque.

Epicaris, the freedwoman turned rebel, towers above the mediocrities who plot against their emperor. She once loved Néron, but that feeling turned to hatred as his growing vices gradually turned him into a monster (1730–44). From the moment of that realization, her one passion became an all-consuming love of liberty, one that erased all other considerations, thus isolating her from her more human co-conspirators. Of common birth, a former slave, Epicaris has in her the heroic spark that allows her to teach Néron the true meaning of *générosité.* "I will not betray such generous hearts" (1705), she tells the tyrant, accentuating his impotence vis-à-vis her steadfastness with "I would die a hundred times before naming them" (1712).

In her final confrontation with the imperial couple, she not only shows her heroic mettle, but also that she has not completely purged herself of her origins—a trait that heightens the dramatic impact, though in a way which was certainly not appreciated by the purists of the age of Louis XIV:

Néron: Do you take pleasure in being tortured?
Epicaris: Less than a tyrant does in ordering it.
Sabine: Impudence! How can Earth stand to bear such a monster?
Epicaris: It can easily carry Epicaris if it can stand the wife of three husbands.
Sabine: For that word your tongue will be cut out.
Epicaris: What should be cut off Sabina Poppaea?
Sabine: Had you vomited that word only you would die a hundred deaths by my command.
Epicaris: I disdain that sort of fear: threaten me rather with life under your reign. No other misfortune could bother me; and that is the only fear that can make me tremble.

When Néron finally interferes in the duel of wits, he too emerges scathed by Epicaris's tongue:

Néron: That's too much! Let her be handed over to the inhuman executioners.
Epicaris: That's a job worthy of Néron's hands.
Néron: Drag her away, soldiers, and let her be torn apart.
Epicaris: Your fate will perhaps be worse one day.
Néron: Wicked one, they will teach you how to discourse.
Epicaris: Tyrant, I will teach you that I know how to die well.
Néron: Let her be killed in the most cruel torments.
Epicaris: Let nothing keep you from your work. (1713–26, 1745–52.)

Note that Sabine's last retort, in spite of her "my command," has no effect on Epicaris who, having dismissed Néron's wife with her "cutting" remark, henceforth concentrates on the tyrant, her real foe. She goes to her death with grandiose rage and pride, escaping the tyrant's clutches and the morass of his topsy-turvy world in the only way possible. If she can no longer hope to live well, then at least she will die well.

Sabine Popée, wife of Néron, is also his evil spirit, his Iago. She has fought hard, and changed beds frequently, but at last she is "without rival," since Octavia, her imperial predecessor, has been eliminated (1–2). Unlike Octavia, who censured Néron's evil evolution, Sabine revels in it and encourages it, her boundless cupidity for wealth and power making her seek out for eradication anyone of wealth or independent spirit. Totally given over to self-gratification, she is a shrewd and convincing advocate, playing with Néron's megalomania and thirst for approbation. As such, her role in the play is of the utmost importance, though she has few momentous, quotable lines. On the other hand, whenever she tries to match a protagonist in a verbal duel, she is easily crushed, as in the above cited confrontation with Epicaris.

Despite the fact that he owes so much of his dynamism to his grey eminence, Néron is a most interesting figure. He is, of course, a megalomaniac and, as such, demands constant and universal approval. Octavia's virtue and disapproval led to her demise and Sabine's rise to favor. The very fact that he owes respect and gratitude to his mentor Sénèque contributes to that noble old man's death. Whatever struggle there is within Néron on that score, is due exclusively to his concept of duty to his imperial image: what will people say? As he creates new values to make his twisted path easier to tread, Néron manufactures a new language and logic to defend these. As he speaks and acts, he erects a façade and words begin to lose their meaning. This becomes evident as of the first scene: "To ruin him more readily, we must caress him. We must set a trap with such artifice that our own trickery will be imputed to him; he must be wrapped in a net so subtle that he will catch himself in it while thinking to evade it, and good people, deceived by appearances, seeing him perish, will blame his own imprudence" (128–34).

Along with absolute power, Néron wants universal approval. He is thus surprised—unlike Hérode, who knew himself shut out from the start—and hurt when he sees the hostility grow as his policies and those of his wife alienate the very ones whose approbation he wants most. The entire first act is taken up almost exclusively with a dialectic which reveals that he is far from secure in his own feelings about his past and present misdeeds, and resents Epicaris not only for "betraying" him (747–50), but even more for voicing the general discontent in Néron's realm (1709–10). Epicaris dies, in effect, because she refuses to relinquish the right to judge the imperial couple.

When, on the heels of Epicaris's dying curse, he hears of Sénèque's stoic death and repudiation of him, Néron is shaken and unable to recover (1846–47). He senses his error, the general condemnation, and feels the furies invading his mind (1850–53). Only Sabine remains faithful, but Néron realizes at last that she is of no use to him and he dismisses her threateningly (1861–63). As the play ends, he is totally alone, simultaneously confronting destiny and his inner self; he reaches his poetic and dramatic potential in his last lines in which he hurls to the heavens the challenge of a man who knows that he is doomed: "O Heaven! who wishes me ill and whom I want to challenge, no one can escape the traps you set: you prepare some thunderbolts for me, but I will first lay half the earth to waste" (1865–68).

Sénèque, having educated Néron to be a proper ruler (179), now finds that his pupil has warped all his teachings and made the earth unfit to live in. At first, he merely seeks to be left alone while the rest of the world goes on its mad way: "Leave your servant in peace . . . to seek relaxation in a pastoral setting where, far from noises and crowds I might quietly consult my books" (192–200). When Néron's madness makes this humble dream impossible, when he realizes that vice has completely taken over his world—a realization he voices in some of the most beautiful *stances* in Tristan's theater—he begins to turn his eyes toward the next world.

It is here that Tristan introduces a startling—but by no means impossible—idea, that of a Seneca ready to convert to Christianity. To be sure, he welcomes death as a source of "eternal peace" (1442), but it is more: it is also the path to a "better life" (1441). To this "liberating God," whom he acknowledges as his prime mover, he offers his soul:

> Voici ce que je t'offre, ô Dieu libérateur.
> Dieu, dont le nouveau bruit a mon âme ravie,
> Dieu, qui n'es rien qu'amour, esprit, lumière et vie,
> Dieu de l'homme de Tharse, où je mets mon espoir,
> Mon âme vient de toi, veuille la recevoir. [19] (1834–38.)

Mariane withdrew from a world that was no longer hers and died rather than accept its values. Sénèque goes to his death with greater serenity because it is a positive step towards regaining those values he can no longer find in this life. In the end, transcending the tragic mode, he finds not only freedom, but a happiness for which his virtuous philosophy has prepared him, one which he knew this world could never give him. This positive ending for a man whose stoicism had previously led more to passive pleasures is given an earthly counterpoint in the last scene between Sénèque and his wife Pauline. At first, he is rather reticent in his declaration of love: he was faithful and without reproach in his affection (1559–61). Pauline's rejoinder is far more impassioned and the ensuing duet grows in exaltation as the two recall their love and devotion, the scene reaching a poetic intensity seldom found in the seventeenth century. Together, they decide to die, praising each other, but above all, praising their new-found God of "love, spirit, light, and life" (1835). This is more than the rejection of an absurdity—it is total commitment to an ideal, one for which Sénèque's philosophy could prepare him, but which it could not get him to attain by itself. It is the news of this death that so shakes Néron's mind, for he knows that in spite of Sabine, whom he shrugs off, he is now truly alone in the mad world he has fashioned.

VI   La Mort de Chrispe

In September, 1644, Tristan gave *La Mort de Chrispe* to the actors of the Illustre Théâtre, then subsidized—badly—by Gaston d'Orléans. The subject had been a rather popular one with minor authors throughout the early part of the century, and Tristan may have had hopes of thus assuring himself of a success. In actuality, the play was a failure. Granted, there were three editions during Tristan's few remaining years, but two of these came out simultaneously in Toulouse and were probably not seen by the author. The tragedy remained in the repertoire for some time, but with rather infrequent and badly attended performances.

The plot is quite simple, but to fully understand its ramifications and to perceive Tristan's innovations, a glance at the historical setting is warrented. During his campaign in Persia and Egypt, Constantine had met Minervina, made her his concubine, and had a son, Chrispus, by her, probably in 307 A.D. In that year, he married Fausta, the daughter and sister of his two greatest rivals for power. In 310 A.D., Fausta revealed to her husband an attempt by her relatives to poison him. Her father was killed immediately and her brother two years later. By 323, Constantine was at war with a brother-in-law with whom he had shared the throne. Chrispus, in spite of his youth, distinguished himself in battle to such an extent that his father became jealous. In 324, Fausta accused Chrispus of having made improper advances; Constantine had him arrested and put to death.

When Constantine's mother revealed her grandson's innocence and Fausta's guilt, Constantine had the latter drowned.

A jealous and barbaric father, and a wanton stepmother such as the one described by the historians, would obviously have disgusted Tristan's public. Major changes were therefore in order. Fauste, who is about twenty-six years old, is in love with her stepson, a "charming idol" of seventeen who, in turn, loves and is loved by Constance. The jealous Fauste decides to rid herself of Constance by sending her a pair of poisoned gloves. The plan backfires when Chrispe smells the gloves and shares Constance's fate. Constantine, upon learning the truth, orders Fauste's death.

As in *La Mariane*, much of the drama is centered on the wall erected by one person to shut out another. The basic difference, of course, is that Hérode and Mariane needed each other, while such is not the case here: whereas Fauste needs Chrispe, he, with a throng of friends and a love of his own, has no use for her at all. There is no question of estrangement for him; a perfectly normal youth, he has no intention of allowing Fauste's stifling passion to invade his world. All her attempts to speak of her love will simply be met by a wall of indifference and incomprehension. There is another difference: in *La Mariane*, Hérode made vehement efforts to breach the wall erected by Mariane; as her husband, he had every right to do so. Fauste's love is patently illegal and immoral, of which she is only too aware; as a result, her efforts are hampered by her own conscience and consciousness; if she remains outside of Chrispe's world of young love, it is as much through her reticence as because of Chrispe's rejection.

There are only two characters of any dramatic import in this play, Chrispe and Fauste: Constance's role is politically ambiguous—being the daughter of one of Constantine's foes, she represents the opposition—however dramatically insignificant. The role of Constantine is barely more than incidental. Tristan, obviously unwilling to put on stage the same bloodthirsty tyrant that history presented, merely has him an august presence commenting on the drama that surrounds him. Even his final order for Fauste's death is somewhat superfluous: since Fauste had already decided to kill herself, he merely gives an official sanction to her decision.

For that matter, Chrispe is interesting only insofar as Fauste makes him so. His serenity is the natural foil for his stepmother's guilty secret, and it is in their interviews that he truly comes to dramatic life.[20]

In short, Fauste and her illicit passion are the focus of this drama improperly entitled "The Death of Chrispus or the Domestic Misfortunes of the Great Constantine." Fauste is torn between duty and love: "This crime makes me simultaneously shudder and burn; reason chastizes me, and my love oppresses me" (41–42). It is only by a supreme effort of will that she renounces any intention of declaring that love, however painful such a decision might be (57–59). However, this resolve will always weaken in the presence of Chrispe's "lovable charms" (57), though unlike Racine's Phèdre, she is too modest to ever fully reveal herself openly.

The curtain rises on her resolve to stifle her love; but no sooner is that voiced than Chrispe is announced and unwisely admitted into her presence. She then, like Phèdre, tries to disguise her declaration of love, expecting to yield to a hoped-for retaliatory declaration. She begins with a song of praise of the dashing hero and of his deeds, this "God," this "immortal" (85–88), but Chrispe totally misunderstands her and turns her compliments into praise of Constantin, hoping thus to please the wife—for he has a favor to ask, help for Constance and her family. Feeling pangs of jealousy, Fauste grows slightly bolder: is there nothing that Chrispe might wish for himself? The innocent youth does not grasp the meaning of the subtle words, and when he continues his flattery, Fauste in turn keeps up the ironic *doubles-entendres:* "Do you wish to seduce me with your flattery?" (283). The scene goes on in this vein, she casting hints, he failing to understand them, until the act ends with his final, optimistic—yet loaded with sinister implications—"I will assume full responsibility" (306). He has unwittingly cast the fatal die and, by his obstinacy, his optimism, his exclusive love, his obliviousness to Fauste's terrible inner struggle, has managed to remain a total stranger to the tragic events that engulf his world. His impermeability—as much if not more than Fauste's reticence—causes the first of a series of misunderstandings and *quid pro quos*, the last of which will be his own absurdly unwanted and unnecessary death.

In the beautiful and touching *stances* that open Act II, Fauste voices her problem:

> Fauste, à quoi te résoudras-tu
> Entre l'amour et la vertu
> Qui tiennent aujourd'hui ton âme balancée?
> Déjà la crainte et le désir

> Font des ligues dans ta pensée;
> Il faut laisser ou prendre, il est temps de choisir.[21] (307–12.)

Her inclination is to yield to peril, but it is only when jealousy is added to her love that she becomes a vengeful fury, assuming in her blind rage that she has been wronged by the young lovers (389–92). It might be argued that Fauste has a right to see in Constance an enemy of the state, and can therefore view Chrispe's love as illegitimate; but too many of her declarations show that this tack is merely a subterfuge on her part. When Constance speaks of her father's crimes against the state, Fauste is quick to point out that the daughter has done worse: the father has sinned against the empire; by loving Chrispe and inciting him to love her, Constance has sinned against Fauste (1159–74). There follows a vitriolic exchange (1191–1200) reminiscent of the one between Sabine and Epicaris, which ends also with an allusion by Constance to Fauste's unsavory past (1200); it is of course this parting sally that seals her fate.

For all that, it should not be thought that anger is Fauste's prime mover—it merely reinforces her already overpowering passion: "She still lives after having attacked my reputation and my love? . . . Rather than let that love offend me without punishment, I will simultaneously ruin both lovers" (1209–42). It is the strength of this passion that allows Fauste to justify herself to herself. Reveling in the joy of her rival's anticipated death, she is fooled by her own dialectics and loses all sense of shame, right and wrong: "By thinking of offending me, Constance has doomed herself. The death she now receives is a deserved punishment" (1403–04). When she learns of the death of the lovers in each other's arms—a death that forever unites them and shuts her out (1551–66)—she does not voice a single word of remorse; rather, it is frustration that she vents, seeing in the dying lovers' last kiss a supreme insult to her own love. She then seeks death not as an end to her misery, but as a means to attempt once more to pursue her rival and spoil her triumph (1567–76).

The play, which has some beautiful tirades—notably *stances*—and some quite dramatic scenes, failed, and deservedly so. The role of Constantin, as I have already said, is episodic and of little consequence. Constance has one lyrical moment and a brief dramatic one, but she is not sufficiently delineated to really become the focus of the public's sympathy; she interests us only insofar as she is Chrispe's beloved. But Chrispe himself plays a rather limited role, for he is a static character, either impervious or passive on stage. Fauste is, therefore, the only interesting character in the entire play, devoid of any worthy foil.

Compounding this weakness is another one, at least as serious. In his efforts to make history and these historic figures more palatable, Tristan had to alter the basic facts; but he did so to the detriment of the play's action. Fauste is not allowed to explicitly declare herself. Her inner turmoil, though touching indeed, is not interesting enough to bear constant repetition. Some of her tirades must strike the reader as tiresome padding. Chrispe's death is no longer imputed directly to either Fauste (the cause) or to Constantin (the agent), but is now little more than an unfortunate accident attributable only indirectly to his stepmother. Constantin, free of this moral burden, becomes a self-righteous father wronged by fate and a wicked wife, while the guilt of the latter is also greatly diminished. Unfortunately, the expurgation also affected the dramatic intensity that might have pervaded the play, a mistake that Racine was careful to avoid in his handling of the same theme.

VII   Osman

Sometime late in 1646 or early in 1647, Tristan finished his last tragedy, *Osman,* and took out an unusually long copyright (*privilège*)—twenty years—in June, 1647. One would suspect that such a protracted protection—five to ten years being the norm—meant that Tristan expected a long and successful series of perform-ances and editions, but such was not the case. In fact, there is no record of any performance, anywhere. Only two contemporaries make mention of the play at all, and not in connection with a performance. For reasons that remain a mystery to this day, Tristan buried the play which was not published until after his death, by his admirer and protégé, Quinault, a fairly good dramatist himself.

Contemporary subjects were not unknown on the French stage, though English and Scottish ones seem to have predominated, but Tristan had not attempted to treat any. The brilliant rise of the Ottoman Empire and its opening of diplomatic relations with the rest of Europe had made it a popular topic of both conversation and literature. Tristan could not help but be familiar with the matter, having probably read Victoria Siri's *Mercurio*, dedicated to Gaston d'Orléans, and other works such as Michel Baudier's very popular

Histoire générale du Sérail. It is also likely that he personally met M. de Cézy, French ambassador to the Porte, a charming conversationalist and raconteur, whose delectable stories of Turkish life opened all doors for him. The stormy history of this new power was, therefore, well known to all and a "natural" for Tristan to treat.

When Sultan Achmet-Khan I died in 1617, his oldest son was only thirteen years old. The deceased's brother, Mustapha, who had spent fourteen years in prison—a procedure considered normal in seventeenth-century Turkey, to preserve peace by preventing factionalism—was put on the throne. Mustapha's prolonged internment, however, had so undermined his already questionable sanity that his reign was shortlived: though some leaders wished to retain him so as to rule through him, others prevailed; and in 1618, Osman, not yet fourteen years old, rose to the throne. In spite of his youth, he appears to have been a fairly good ruler, and the military genius of his Grand Vizier, Khalil-Pasha, undoubtedly helped his rising popularity.

After Khalil-Pasha's victories in Persia, Osman's victorious campaigns against Poland and Venice consecrated the young Sultan's glory. In 1621, he had his brother strangled, again, a then normal procedure designed to prevent factionalism. But problems began to arise. A brutal winter caused a severe famine; Osman's cupidity, his arrogance, his severity vis-à-vis his Janissaries, his constant reliance on external campaigns to take attention away from internal problems —to the point where he attempted to levy an army in Asia to supplement (or supplant?) his Janissaries—all these matters led to widespread discontent. Deeply religious, he made public a desire to go on a pilgrimage to Mecca. The Janissaries, fearing a ruse by which Osman would join his Egyptian troops and thus end the Janissaries' control of military affairs, rebelled. Osman disguised himself and tried to escape. Captured, he was thrown in jail where, in spite of his youthful tears, the teenaged ruler was strangled.

In his treatment of the story, Tristan remained fairly faithful to history. Osman's avarice and piety are omitted, and his death is a fierce and noble one, Osman fighting to the end to prevent his capture. Tristan invented the role of Osman's sister, and gave a primary one to an obscure historic figure, the Mufti's daughter, a girl in love with Osman. In the play, it is this scorned woman who sets off the brewing rebellion. To safeguard the unity of action, he reduced to insignificance the roles of the influential Mufti, of the Grand Vizier, and of Mustafa, the mad uncle declared "saintly" by those who would rule through him when they put him back on the throne after Osman's death.

Tristan was also faithful to the unities, by then well entrenched, though he opted for a variation then beginning to be used, one which Racine was to bring to full fruition: usage demanded a single action to which some minor side issues could be grafted if they contributed to the elucidation of the main one. Here, Tristan gives us two parallel ones, the political struggle of Osman and the erotic one of the Mufti's daughter, both inseparably intertwined into a single entity that can only be loosened by death. As a result, more than any other play by Tristan—and therein lies its major interest for any student of that author—*Osman* is the tragedy of a human being "alone and impotent before destiny, alone and unhappy before men."[22]

I have stated earlier that Tristan created the role of Osman's sister. Yet, he never gave her a name. She is omnipresent in the early scenes, though identified only as "*La Sultane Soeur*," and disappears midway through Act II, reappearing only momentarily in Act IV, scene 2, to announce the rebellion. Furthermore, as some critics have noted, she lacks personality. All that is true, but for a very good reason. At no time is she allowed to participate in the tragic action, however great her love and concern for her brother may be. She sees—the play opens with her startled awakening from a dream in which she has observed her brother being killed—and bemoans. In the tragic world of Tristan—as in all great Classical tragedies—the gods are called upon, but they seldom answer. Fate rules by inconsistency and caprice, a truth first enunciated by the sister (333) and echoed, however belatedly, by Osman (1243).

The gods, then, do not answer those who seek to know; but ironically, they do grant a vision to a few witnesses of the human drama, one which only enhances their misery and estrangement. The Sultane Soeur, with her vision of the future, is, to repeat Dalla Valle's perceptive statement, alone and impotent before destiny and, sole believer in the content of her vision, alone and unhappy before men. She bears initially and painfully the nuclei of the tragic action. Once these have been embodied in Osman and the Fille du Mouphti, this Ottoman Cassandra is no longer necessary, and so disappears.

Like Mariane, Osman finds himself a stranger in his own land. Proud of his birth and his ability to live up to its expectations, he is bitterly disappointed in all his human relations. Justifiably or not, he finds his Janissaries so lacking in fighting spirit that they remind him of eunuchs (118) willing to be slaughtered like "brutish beasts" (123). Instead of valor, he sees only intrigue. Even in love he is disillusioned: having seen a portrait of the Fille du Mouphti, he falls in love with her with the same youthful ardor he demonstrates in all his other endeavors, only to find the girl's attributes falling far short of the picture's promise. Ironically, Osman, who will succumb because of his excessive pride, objects primarily to precisely that attribute in her: "She has twenty times more pride than beauty" (435). Like Mariane, Osman cannot reconcile the notion he has of what people should be with the examples before his eyes and with whom he has nothing in common. His decision to join his army in Egypt is due less to political exigencies than to frustration, since he hopes to find there men who still feel as he does about battle (141–48). When this avenue is cut off, it is not merely men he must face, but his destiny as well.

From the start, the young ruler is aware of his station (159–60), and he knows how to use the power he derives therefrom. He expects to strike fear in all (222) and is utterly confident of his mastery over his subjects and of his ability to shape his destiny and theirs. He soon finds out—and lucidly faces the fact—that he is alone (934). The Fille du Mouphti who tries repeatedly to enter into his world, is rejected by the brutal idealist. His loneliness is accentuated by the fact that, although his bravery is essential and hereditary—"The honor of our ancestors whose greatness still shines in our eyes" is the beacon of this *généreux* (991–92)—his sister, however, does not share it, showing, instead a weakness Osman considers to be an unworthy degeneration (1026). As is obvious, this loneliness is maintained solely by the sheer will of a man who refuses the human contacts repeatedly proffered. Even the rebellion could be avoided or squashed. His Janissaries seek only a brief audience (1115); but he rejects their request out of pure pride, asking them what makes them think that they can advise or dictate (1083–84). His values never change, his resolve never wavers. Cruelly truthful to the end—see his ultimate insult to the Fille du Mouphti, whose love he finds more of a curse than his ills (1338–42)[23]—he accepts his assured death (1396) and exits like a sultan, his honor and his isolation intact.

One of the great creations of Tristan, worthy counterpart of Osman, is the Fille du Mouphti. Even as he rejects her for falling short of matching her flattering portrait, Osman is struck by her proud bearing (428–35). Rejected and shamefully dismissed, the jilted young lady assumes an attitude that has led many critics to liken her to Racine's Hermione: "Vengeance shall be mine. All good

Moslems, angels, men, heavens and elements will be against him, and were I alone set on his death, he would better know that his life is far from secure" (482–86). With Selim, a malcontent, she plots to topple Osman from the throne she had hoped to share, promising to personally reward him once the task is completed (555–60). Though she tells Selim, "I will know your heart when I see his head" (558), she, like Hermione plotting with Oreste, knows that she cannot reward Selim, since her heart is no longer hers (648). In spite of her well-nurtured hatred, co-existent with it is a love for Osman that she is forced to admit after a thorough self-examination (655–74), and which she sets aside only with the greatest of efforts to pursue a vengeance she now views as a sacred duty (702).

Dramatically and poetically, the Fille du Mouphti exists only on the erotic level. Her plotting is indecisive, though it sets off the already simmering rebellion. Therefore, Tristan keeps her off stage throughout the fourth act, while Osman fights for his throne. Only in the last act, when that battle has been decided, does she reappear, as torn as ever. Pride and hurt love make a reconciliation impossible. What should have been a declaration of love is made to sound like gratuitous reproaches. When she prolongs this tirade (1319–37), Osman's brutal rejection seems almost justified. During the stichomythic duel that ensues (1337–42), she is forced to retreat. Realizing the error of her initial approach, she changes course, admitting that her gloating deserved his rejoinder. This "crime," however, was due to hurt pride and, even more, as she points out, to love. In lines of supreme beauty, she pours out her heart, demonstrating in the process that, since she loves him now that he is fallen, her love could not have been motivated by ambition: "I loved Osman himself, and not the emperor, and I considered in your noble person gems of another price than those of your crown" (1374–76). Were she now queen and he a common soldier, "He would have but to love me and everything would be his" (1382). Osman is touched by this passion which he discovers too late. His mind is no longer on love, but on survival, or at least on his duty to himself. Proud to the end, he rejects her offer to hide him in her rooms. Again he couches his rejection in such forceful terms—more than anything else to inure himself against her increasingly manifest virtues—that the hapless Fille du Mouphti must come to grips with the sad truth that she will always love him, while he will never return the sentiment: "He cannot stand me, he hates me, he abhors me, he leaves me, runs from me, and yet I love him still" (1403–04). By the time she decides to die with him or for him, the glorious but gory death of Osman is announced.

In spite of a somewhat precious and intellectualized dialectic, her last lines are the poetic and dramatic distillation of this tortured being. Though she has just been told that Osman's severed head is being paraded at the end of a pike, she declares that he is not dead, since she is alive (1586). "He flows through my blood, he courses through my mind; with all his insolence, with all his injustice, he remains in my heart; but he must die. And he will die this instant, this beloved man who could only die by my hand" (1600–04). Stabbing herself repeatedly, she simultaneously ends her life and "his." With "the deed is done" twice on her lips, she finally exorcises her two warring passions. Unlike Fauste, she does not pursue her lover; she frees herself from him and, like Mariane, finds peace.

It may well be that *Osman* was never performed; and it is probably well that, as long as there is a *Bajazet* with which it would inevitably be compared, it never be performed. But the poetry, the magnificent pomp of the tirades, do not deserve to be buried and forgotten. More important yet, whether one wishes to see Tristan as a writer in his own rights, or as a precursor of Racine, in *Osman,* he managed to create an atmosphere as no one had done before, and as only Racine was to do after him. From the first line of the Sultane Soeur's nightmare to the Fille du Mouphti's dying gasp, the reader with imagination and sensitivity is immersed in a claustrophobic and stifling atmosphere such as the one that must have prevailed in the Seraglio. The barbaric grandeur echoed by the sonorous alexandrines, the ominous mystery of court intrigues, the passions engendered by human beings who consider human life an expendable commodity, all this is part of a psychological mantle that covers the empathetic reader and grants him—through this feeling of barbarity—a further understanding of the human experience.

CHAPTER 8

The Comic Muse

I *Burlesque*

LIKE all the poets of his time, Tristan sacrificed to the comic muse, and if we are to believe his contemporaries, did so extensively. But—perhaps because he did not hold that production in high esteem—he seldom signed these works and, as a result, many of those attributed to his pen can be done so only with the greatest reserve. If one is to judge by those of his works in that vein which are signed, and whose authorship is beyond doubt, he was quite right to disown the bulk of that production, for it fails to reach levels of excellence set either by his other works or by the burlesque poems of contemporaries such as Saint-Amant and Scarron. Still, Tristan's comic verses do not altogether deserve oblivion. Besides his three comic plays and the libretti of several court ballets, there are a few burlesque poems that stand up well under comparative scrutiny, and these are worthy of attention and comment.

Almost all the forms normally associated with serious endeavors were used at one time or another by Tristan in his satiric or burlesque sallies. What is even more remarkable is that, in his parodic efforts, he used prosodic processes which his contemporaries reserved exclusively for their more serious efforts. Thus, the metaphors, *pointes* and conceits, and the sustained images, are as frequent in his *badinages* as in his most serious endeavors. This is, in fact, the source of much of the comicality that imbues these poems.

The opening of "La Gouvernante importune" (*Amours*) has the bite of a Régnier satire:

> Vieux singe au visage froncé
> De qui tous les pages se rient,
> Et dont le seul nom prononcé
> Fait taire les enfants qui crient,
> Vieux simulacre de la Mort,

Qui nous importunes si fort
Par le chagrin de ta vieillesse;
A parler sans déguisement,
Le temps avec trop de paresse
Te traîne au monument.[1]

Calling her an old crow who has seen with her own eyes all that is
chronicled in history, a rotten skeleton seemingly risen from the
earth, he justifies his angry diatribes by pointing out that it is the hag's
presence that makes the Graces and Love languish, and laughter and
pleasure stop and flee like frightened birds. The very excesses of
these diatribes have a certain comicality about them, but the real
genius of Tristan is demonstrated by his taking the clichés of *précieux*
poetry and applying them in a distorted fashion: the "immortal
Graces" find themselves juxtaposed with "a cold and colorless
virtue," sighs of despair are heard not because a young lady will not
pay attention to him, but because the governess *does*, shedding
"inopportune light" on the trysting place. To the careful reader of
Tristan, it quickly becomes apparent that the poet readily saw that
the height of parody was self-parody.

The best burlesque poems of Tristan can all be viewed as
mirrors—however distorting—of his serious poems, both erotic and
heroic. As such, they shed an important light on his production. Even
the seemingly insignificant mock epitaphs are clever distortions of
the real ones:

Ici gît un buveur dont l'âme était ravie
Lorsqu'il se remplissait de vin vieux ou nouveau;
Je crois qu'il n'aurait point de regret à sa vie
Si quelques muids en perce étaient en son caveau.[2]
(*Vers héroïques*, "Tombeau d'un ivrogne de qualité.")

The "Epitre burlesque" (*Vers héroïques*), sent to a young poetess, is a
delightful parody of the "guirlande" type of poem, Tristan here
dressing the girl in poems of different types, the laughter deriving
from the very imaginative enumerative process, a procedure Tristan
will refine in the tirades of Fripesauces and Le Capitan of his
Parasite. No less parodic is the witty description of the torments of
the lover kept at bay by an adamant doorkeeper in "Le Portier
inexorable" (*Amours*). The irritable countenance of the guard,
inflamed by wine, leads the frustrated lover to exclaim: "Gods, to
make my torment eternal, will you not have Cerberus guard my love

since this doorman suffices to guard Hell?" Undoubtedly, the most polished of these burlesque poems is the sonnet "Le Ravissement d'Europe" (*Plaintes*). The subject matter—the abduction of Europa, daughter of the King of Sidon, by Jupiter who, disguised as a bull, carries her off to his island of Crete—is treated in fairly elevated tones until the final tercet, when Neptune, who has been watching the terrified Europa cling to the bull's horns, is made to exclaim: "Inconstant one, who cannot be kept by a single love, since you wish to have horns in spite of your wife Juno, why doesn't she resolve to give you a set?"[3]

Not all the burlesque poems of Tristan are of that caliber. His burlesque liminary poems, patently dashed off in a hurry, have a forced wit; and if at times the undeniable skill of the poet shows through, it is not enough to redeem them. Some of his satiric digs can be excessively cruel, as when he wrote to a surgeon who had just married a rather old woman: "If you wed this antique skeleton to hang it in your shop, I cannot say that you were wrong; but why, beautiful serenader, do you want to sleep in death's bed before you are buried?" (*Vers héroïques*, "Pour un chirurgien qui épousait une vieille femme"). The "Prosopopée d'un singe," from the same collection, ends with the monkey telling an ugly little painter, "An imitator of your kind is nothing but a monkey like me." However, "Pour un parasite" (*Vers héroïques*), ten satiric lines about a pedantic parasite, are as witty as any penned in the genre:

> Ce pédant parasite au visage égaré,
> Veut qu'on serve sur table à même temps qu'il entre,
> Et tout ce qu'il avale est plus tôt digéré
> Que s'il avait cent loups enragés dans le ventre.
> La faim dans ses boyaux murmure incessamment;
> On ne pourrait trouver un monstre plus gourmand
> Quand on le chercherait de l'un à l'autre pole;
> Bref il est transporté d'un désir si glouton
> Qu'il mordit une fois un passant à l'épaule
> A cause qu'il sentait l'épaule de mouton.[4]

There is another aspect of Tristan's burlesque production that is seldom discussed: its obscenity, best seen in his libretti for courtly ballets, a relatively shortlived genre, born in October, 1581, with the creation at court of the *Ballet comique de la Reine* ("*comique*" meaning "dealing with theater"). As a spectacular distraction for rich amateurs, it eventually yielded to its various offspring (*opéra-ballet*, *comédie-ballet*, professional ballet with its more intricate and difficult steps removed from the dances performed by all at court). The genre, to which Tristan contributed in the 1620's and 1630's, is a combination of poetry, dance, stagecraft, and song, some lines sung by a chorus, some by soloists, most of them simply recited by the wealthy and powerful amateurs to explain the meaning and/or symbolism of their dances. Subservient to the music, the staging, and the lavish costuming that allowed these touchy egos to parade, the poetry was usually commissioned and written at the last minute after all the other, more "important" aspects of the spectacle had been set, and printed as handbills. These were not only prized by the spectators, but also by those less fortunate for whom every aspect of court entertainment was Gospel for conversation and emulation.

But if they were prized, it was not for their poetic merit, which is invariably nonexistent, and Tristan's contribution to the genre is no exception. As a member of Gaston's court—one as libertine as any—Tristan wrote ballet libretti as obscene as any, as this sample indicates:

> Belles qui pour tenir plus nets
> Les lambris de vos cabinets,
> Balayez et fête et dimanche,
> Venez à moi, je vous promets
> De vous accomoder d'un manche
> Qui ne se cassera jamais.[5]

In Tristan's days, burlesque poetry was expected to be as artificial as its most *précieux* counterpart. A parody of the nobler genres, burlesque undermined those poets who took themselves too seriously and the amateurs who worshipped at their temples. With Tristan, as with most of his brothers-in-arms, such a parody—which, at its best, is self-parody—is more frequently mischievous, rather than nasty. It seeks neither to reform nor to destroy, but rather to mock an elevation which, by its omnipresence, invited, if not laughter, at least a derisive smile. The Tristan we can discern in his best burlesque poems is a lucid artist before his mirror. The oxymora, the antitheses, the metaphors—in short, the entire arsenal of this burlesque poet—was borrowed from his serious alter ego. That is its genius, and half of its charm.

II   La Folie du sage

Published in 1645, *La Folie du sage*, Tristan's only tragi-comedy, is an anomaly in more ways than that. Tragi-comedy, a mixed genre, corresponded to the taste of the public, gaining its greatest popularity between 1633 and 1635. After that, a rapid decline is discernible, corresponding to an equal rise in the popularity of comedy and tragedy. In 1645, only five tragi-comedies appeared; in 1649, when *La Folie* was enjoying its fourth edition, only two new tragi-comedies appeared. After that date, performances got fewer and fewer, and the play sank rapidly into oblivion. Why did this rather mediocre play, obviously flying against the change of the winds, gain such popularity when everything—including its own merits—militated against it?

It is not without danger to trace parallels between a work of art and the milieu whence it came; but in this case, I believe that such an endeavor is worthwhile for the light it sheds on some of the themes and the ephemeral success of *La Folie*. Normally, tragi-comedy shied away from history to transport readers and viewers into a never-never land. Tristan situated his play in a nearby land, Sardinia, and filled it with allusions to contemporary events. Why?

In 1631, Gaston d'Orléans, Tristan's patron, rebelled against his royal brother and fled to Lorraine, where he sought refuge at the court of the powerful duke. When he married the duke's sister, Marguerite de Vaudémont, Louis XIII besieged the city, and Gaston was forced to flee to Bruxelles where he raised an army with the help of the Spaniards. Invading France, he was defeated and returned to Bruxelles, but continued his relations with the court of Lorraine where he had left his wife. When Louis XIII besieged Nancy, the capital of Lorraine, Marguerite, fearing for her life, disguised herself and fled alone, on horseback, to Bruxelles. Louis XIII tried repeatedly to have the marriage annulled, but Gaston, to show his good faith and steadfast intentions, went through a second marriage ceremony with Marguerite and had the marriage validated by the Pope and the theologians of Louvain. By 1633, Gaston, repeatedly defeated in battle, was forced to return to France, leaving his wife in the Spanish Lowlands. The unfortunate couple would not be reunited until 1643, at the death of Louis XIII.

La Folie du sage is just as melodramatic as the events I have just related, but its plot far from parallels the story of Gaston and Marguerite. The King of Sardinia tells Ariste that he loves his daughter Rosélie and wants her for his mistress. Ariste rebuffs his sovereign, but the latter only enlists the aid of his friend Palamède to press his suit, unaware that Palamède and Rosélie love each other. Palamède tries to dissuade the King, but only succeeds in transforming the passion into an honorable one: the King sends Palamède to ask for Rosélie's hand for him. Rosélie, considering herself alone and betrayed, decides to kill herself. In a note, she cryptically mentions her father and her lover as the causes of her death, and the King turns on them in anger. Ariste loses his mind, but it is discovered that Rosélie has merely taken a sleeping potion and is recovering. When she finds her situation unchanged, she seeks death anew, but the King, impressed and mollified, gives the lovers permission to wed.

Though there is little similarity in plot, the star-crossed lovers of *La Folie* recall those of real life, as does the unflinching resolve of the two women who dare all to preserve their love. Nevertheless, this is not a "pièce à clefs" in which contemporaries were expected to recognize real people behind the masks of fiction. Rather, it presents to these contemporaries situations and events which they could view with a certain familiarity and pleasure of vicarious participation. Such "mirrors" are quite numerous in the play, and a few deserve to be pointed out.

When Canope, the confidante of Rosélie, praises Palamède and his love (321–26), and when Rosélie replies, telling of the King's anger and of the fear this anger has thrown into her father's heart (335–38), who at the time, could fail to recall the fury of Louis XIII and the trepidation of the Duke of Lorraine? When Rosélie tells Palamède of her fears (551–54), and he contemplates rebellion or flight (561–72), how can this fail to ring a bell? In the play, as in real life, the woman is the stronger soul, the more steadfast lover. Tristan had served Gaston for many years without proper reward. In 1644, with the princely couple reunited, he dedicated the play to Marguerite, presumably hoping that she would reward this portrayal of her superior faith, one which, like that of Rosélie, refused to bow to royal and familial pressures. The play was probably composed after Marguerite's reunion with Gaston and her triumphal installation in Paris. It is the dramatization of a love before which even royalty must admit defeat. In the years after the death of Louis XIII, Gaston's star shone with meteoric brilliance, and the play enjoyed great success. With the end of the Fronde, a new king was established in his functions, and Gaston was relegated to his provincial castle of Blois where he was promptly forgotten. So was the play.

Though considerations such as the ones alluded to so far cannot absorb the modern reader for long, *La Folie* is not entirely devoid of interest. Part of this is due to Tristan's use of sources. Aside from the scenes of Ariste's madness—which are perhaps drawn from Tristan's own delirium while he was seriously ill at the siege of Montauban, one of the military experiences related by the former page—and the obvious borrowings from La Calprenède's *Edouard,* there are a fair number of general ideas drawn from contemporary literature. In that sense, *La Folie* is probably Tristan's least original play—if one excepts *Amarillis,* an adaptation of another author's sketch. This impression is due less to specific lines attributable to equally specific sources,[6] than it is to such lines and scenes readily identifiable as commonplaces: the madness of Ariste, and even the specifics of his ramblings—though only Tristan could have given him such learned tirades—which can be found in countless plays of the period;[7] Ariste's rejoinder, when he learns of the King's dishonorable intentions (126–27), which can be found in Shakespeare's *Henry VI, Part 3* (97–98), Alarcon's *Las Paredes oyen* (III, 223–24), *Los Pechos privilegiados* (I, vii, 49–52), and *La Prueba de las promesas* (1377–80); or the theme of the living-dead girl and the sleeping potion's effect on the plot, ploys already old when Tristan used them.[8]

Most interesting in these borrowings is the personal timbre that Tristan impresses on them. Madness pervades the Baroque theater, as it does Tristan's—witness Hérode and Néron—but Ariste's madness is of a special type. Unlike his tragic counterparts, Ariste feels no guilt; his folly is a balm needed by a mind that cannot face too stark a reality; but once the horror is gone, he returns to his former, healthy, state. His access of folly is not merely learned; he has built his entire life around his search for knowledge. Knowledge and virtue are the beacons which are expected to lead him through life. Suddenly, Ariste discovers that virtue can be defeated by fortune and that science, unreliable, has betrayed him. What would all the wise men whose writings extol virtue, and whom he considered infallible mentors, say if they could consider his miserable state (941–76)?[9] Ariste, then, in his momentary madness, not only recalls a personal experience of the young Tristan, but utters thoughts that were central to all of Tristan's writings. Nor is Ariste alone in thinking that virtue is directly opposed by fate. When Rosélie—who, like her father, considers herself blameless in every way—sees her hopes of happiness dashed, she opines that "ill fortune is solely guilty. It is purely the result of the angered stars' envy of my prosperity" (590–92). Ariste agrees: "Under what cruel star was I born . . . what malignant star bringing misery, infusing poison into prosperous things, has suddenly changed my happy state?" (889–95). Though he wonders which gods he may have offended, his question seems more rhetorical than literal: like his daughter, he sees little if any connection between his mode of life and his misfortune.

If man succombs to such forces, it is not exclusively due to the malice of the stars. He must carry within himself the seeds of his destruction, being "a piglet inside, an ape outside, . . . reasonable and laughable, . . . a little universe in which the elements bring a thousand ills and changes . . . a vessel . . . that forever undermines itself and ceaselessly destroys itself," says Ariste (996–1010). In other words, the stars, with the help of that person's own weaknesses, may destroy a person's happiness, but they cannot conquer a stout heart. Ariste's best lines are not his mad ramblings—however interesting these may be—but those spoken during confrontation with a king about to forget his duty:

Le Roi: Suis-je pas souverain?
Ariste: Oui, Sire, et je suis père.
Le Roi: Mais sujet.
Ariste: Mais d'un coeur et trop noble et trop franc

Pour vous prostituer indignement son sang.
....
Le Roi: Vous parlez un peu haut.
Ariste: Je parle avec justice.
Le Roi: Il y va de la vie.
Ariste: Et bien, que je périsse.
Je rendrai pour le moins l'esprit avec l'honneur.[10] (122–31.)

Though the King willingly yields to a new star, one whose influence is irresistible—Rosélie, thus identified in Tristan's usual *précieux* terms—he does not come to grips with this question of personal integrity until he realizes that Rosélie prefers death to union with him (1449–50). It is this contagious realization that leads to the happy conclusion.

Interesting though these aspects may be, they do not redeem a play based too heavily on ambiguities and themes which could only appeal to a limited public for a limited time. The logorrhea, which the seventeenth-century audience thought funny, is no longer considered to be so. The immediate success of the play is readily understandable; so is its fall into oblivion, however interesting a few isolated scenes may be to the specialists.

III   Amarillis

In 1652, yielding to the pleas of friends, Tristan adapted Rotrou's *Célimène*, made a pastoral of it, and thus contributed to a surprising renewal of the genre. The play had a rather brief but definite success, and was even performed at court. It is very likely that Molière tried his hand at pastoral comedy because he saw in the successful *Amarillis* and its imitations an ideal prototype for spectacular court entertainment.

Fickle Tyrène has abandoned his lover Bélise and run off to the country, where he woos Amarillis. Bélise reproaches him and taunts him as an ineffective lover: she will masquerade as a man and succeed where he has failed. He agrees that if she does, he will return to her. Bélise not only succeeds in her attempt, but Amarillis's sister, Daphné, also falls in love with her. When the lovers of the sisters threaten the disguised girl, she promises to reunite them. After several peripeteias—less numerous and more witty than in Rotrou—Bélise reveals her ruse and her true sex—by baring her breasts—and the play ends with a triple reunion.

Tristan did not work from Rotrou's *Célimène* as published, but from a now lost canvas. It is, therefore, impossible to discern all of Tristan's contributions from Rotrou's. Only the *stances* and the scenes involving some delightful satyrs are definitely Tristan's. Judging by what we know of Rotrou's work as it finally saw print, Tristan obviously removed many archaisms, lightened the still clumsy and involved plot, and removed much of what was coarse and vulgar in Rotrou—although the innovations concerning the satyrs are themselves quite risqué, they are redeemed by wit and brilliance.[11]

Aside from these delightful creations, the play has only one other feature of interest to admirers of Tristan, the treatment of constancy. Bélise is constant; Tyrène is not. Bélise is so stable that even her disguise as a man fails to alter her, while in Tyrène, the amatory change is made manifest by an outer one, his disguise as a shepherd (208–13). His sole excuse is that his heart cannot be governed by reason: he recognizes Bélise's merits and the foolishness of his new enterprise: "I agree that I am leaving an incomparable treasure to sow on wind and build on sand" (224–25). Bélise is willing to change in more ways than one (physically) to prove her constant love: in spite of a condescending attitude toward the country (213), she has left Lyon and the Burgundian court—a court she heartily despises (8–9)—and changes herself into a shepherd. It is here that Tristan's cachet is imprinted in a way that brings to mind his best poetry: Bélise's "masks" are worn to deny changes and to reestablish order by destroying other masks—such as Amarillis's avowed indifference to love, or Daphné's basic reticence. As we shall see in *Le Parasite*, Tristan views metamorphosis as the ultimate revealer of reality.

IV   Le Parasite

In 1653, just when the French were getting ready for great comedies of manners and of characters, Tristan—as Racine was to do with his *Plaideurs*—deliberately turned to antiquity and the *commedia dell'arte* for the inspiration of a piece of pure buffoonery perpetrated by caricaturesque archetypes. Ironically, the result, *Le Parasite*, was fairly successful, and maintained itself in the repertory for nearly thirty years. It was last performed in 1683, and then disappeared from the stage until the twentieth century, when it was revived on several occasions with mixed results. Tristan, like Racine, belittled his only comedy, calling it a "little diversion," unworthy of attention. It is easy to dismiss this as a clever device, a ploy of false modesty, but he may have been sincere: the only edition put out in his lifetime is done with extreme carelessness, and Tristan obviously did nothing about it, before or after the first impression.[12]

Unlike its sources, the *Angelica* of Fornaris and the *Olimpia* of Della Porta, *Le Parasite* has a good, clear plot, well developed and devoid of either unnecessary complications or halting moments. Lisandre and Lucinde are in love. To allow his master to see his lady love, the forever rapacious parasite Fripesauces introduces him into her house by claiming that he is her long lost brother—Lucinde's brother and father having been captured by Barbary pirates some twenty years earlier. Le Capitan, a cowardly braggadocio of the first degree, also desires Lucinde and tries his best to prevent the union of Lisandre and Lucinde. The inopportune return of the long lost father almost spoils things, when he is enlisted by the schemers—who do not realize who he is—to portray himself; but in the end the duped parents forgive the children and bless their union.

The plot, mere vehicle for one of the finest examples of the reincarnation of the spirit of the *commedia dell'arte*, is of no consequence. The verbal fantasy unleashed by Le Capitan and Fripesauces—and, to a lesser extent, by the Nurse—the wit and *élan vital*, the old, anachronistic language deliberately abused by Tristan for its comic effect, all these ingredients of a gigantic burlesque feast for the mind are what make *Le Parasite* the delight that it is. The Italian influences, though undeniable, are less those of specific plays than the broad joyous qualities brought to France by the "Italian" players. As a result, though the play deals with young love and its travails, its interest is centered on the movers of the comic action, the parasitic Fripesauces, the *miles gloriosus* Capitan, and the nurse Phenice.

The Nurse had disappeared from the French stage for lack of actors and actresses willing and able to portray her.[13] As in the ancient tradition, Tristan's Phenice is quick to anger and equally quick to be soothed. Cynical, capable, and shrewd, she is willing to do anything to further the cause of the young lovers who, without her, would be lost. As things turn out, her salty verbal assaults and colossal bluffs always suffice. When she does go overboard and verbally abuses a man, who turns out to be her master, her tirade has all the trenchancy of a Régnier satire:

> . . . vieux allebran,
> Simulacre plâtré, antiquaille mouvante,
> Squelette décharné, sépulture ambulante,
> Monopoleur insigne, et maître des larrons,
> De qui les coins des yeux semblent des éperons,
> Et de qui chaque tempe est creusée en saucière . . .[14] (914–19)

When the time comes for recognition—and possible retribution— her quick-witted reversal is both funny and an effective means to a full pardon (1725–26).

Le Capitan is true to the type of the *miles gloriosus*, the boastful but cowardly soldier; and Tristan's inventiveness is manifest, not in the psychology of the character, but in the extravagance of the boastful tirades: "I will wring his neck like a chicken's . . . With one glance strike lightning in his intestines . . . break his sternum and ribs . . . There is no David for a Goliath like me . . ." (654–70). When the man he so threatens appears, Le Capitan, of course, sings an entirely different tune:

Cascaret:	What if it were he [the threatened] coming?
Le Capitan:	He'd find out what size boot I wear.
Lisandre:	Obviously no more than a size twelve.
Capitan:	Unless I've been misinformed, at least fourteen.
Lisandre:	Show us your heels; scoot!

Capitan:	The whole thing is very fine leather.
Lisandre:	I thought I told you to get out of here.
Capitan:	I was leaving.
Lisandre:	It is time to draw blood.
Capitan:	I need mine and know yours. (671–80)

The stichomythic exchange gathers momentum until Le Capitan is thoroughly cowed and, at the mere name of a rival, runs off. The quickest—and funniest—reversal occurs in Act V, scene iv, when the Capitan's threats to turn an entire neighborhood into a gigantic cemetery, to blow up houses, kill entire families along with their pets, and send their ashes flying to the most distant regions of the globe—tirades in which Tristan beautifully unites his knowledge of geography with inimitable verbal fantasy—are suddenly interrupted by his espying of a distant police detachment—and his immediate flight.

The eloquence of Le Capitan is easily matched by that of Fripesauces; but the latter is intent on massacres of a different type: "My knife . . . will create a Saint Bartholomew's massacre in the farm yard. The chicken coop will be the scene of carnage, a barrel will be broken open so that I might swim in wine, nothing will be spared to sate me; I will eat my fill, I mean to the top . . ." (625–30). Unlike the factotum of the *commedia*, a far cry from the servants of Molière who, like Figaro, are able to help the young lovers in their intrigues to salvage their happiness, Fripesauces is totally inept—except when the filling of his cavernous stomach is involved—an ineptitude that is in itself a great source of laughter.

Many of his tirades strike me as parodic, be it of Le Capitan's martial declarations or of the young couple's amorous ones. His last tirade of Act IV is a truly plaintive one, as his heart—stomach?—is breaking. After more than six years of devotion—burning his nose while turning the spit—and all the hard work imaginable for the preparation of a forthcoming feast, he will not be able to participate. His tirade waxes as he curses love and lovers:

> Que maudit soit l'amour et quiconque s'en mêle;
> Au diable le fripon, dont les meilleurs valets
> Ont l'estomac si vide en portant des poulets[15] (1388–90),

but it quickly turns into a tearful farewell to all that he loves: "Farewell beef breast and delightful back plate, farewell beautiful fat

118TRISTAN L'HERMITE

mutton of such delectable taste, farewell roast pigs . . ." (1391–98), a
direct parody of the lovers' farewells, in which the swain was
expected to bid farewell to each aspect of the woman's *blason*.

It is in such delightful spoofs that Tristan is at his comic best; but
many of his funniest sallies must take some of the blame for the play's
eventual demise. The coarse Gallic wit, in which he revels, defies all
the rules of decorum. Although such devices were not entirely
banned from the comic stage, as can be seen by any glance at
Molière's dramatic production, they are altogether too frequent in *Le
Parasite*. For the modern reader, many of these present distinct
problems, as they rely for much of their humor on puns that are no
longer operative. Thus, in one of the recognition scenes, when the
Nurse exclaims, "A-t-il pas tout le haut de sa mère?", Fripesauces
replies, "Mais je crois que du bas il ressemble à son père" (831–32). In
modern French, only a certain risqué allusion remains: "Doesn't he
have his mother's top?" "But I think his lower parts are more his
father's." In the seventeenth century, *haut* meant not only "top" or
"upper part," and "pride" or "proud mien," but—of greater importance to this particular sally—also had the denotation of "lewd-
ness."

Of equal appeal to the original audience was the Baroque predilection for disguise, one which the generation of Molière did not share.
Disguise is prevalent throughout *Le Parasite*, but Tristan saved the
best for last: when the plotters feel the need to have someone
impersonate the missing father, they pick—unwittingly, of course—
the very man to be impersonated himself, just returned from a
prolonged captivity. The best mask is the real thing or, more
specifically, the best disguise is one that creates reality. As
Fripesauces says, when he admires what he thinks is his directorial
masterpiece, "Never did actor better play his role" (1215).

Such twists are not limited to disguises. In the final scenes, the
anger of the fathers makes them blurt out truths which, as shrewd
bourgeois, they would otherwise never divulge. It is these revelations about their property and wealth that make them see the
"propriety" of the marriage that the two young lovers contemplated
all along. As in *La Folie*, madness—in this case, an irrational
anger—is a form of lucidity, a revealer of truth.

As Racine was to do with his only comedy, Tristan belittled *Le
Parasite*, calling it a "little diversion" in his dedication. It is much
more than that: deliberately relying on a language and a framework
both antiquated and base, he used that archaism and verbal fantasy as

sources of laughter in a way unknown since Rabelais, and which only Molière was to resurrect with such gusto. His contribution to comedy is undeniable. He easily outdistanced his predecessors in the relief of his caricaturesque figures and the verve of his poetry. At a time when farce and serious comedy were finally to be merged on stage, he gave verbal fantasy and burlesque its finest hours. This was quite enough to assure—and justify—the meteoric success of the play. However, it was also to spell its doom: the Classical generation, by subduing burlesque, fixing the language, and demanding psychological depth even in its comedy, made a Molière inevitable and *Le Parasite* passé.

CHAPTER 9

Conclusion

I *The Poet*

TRISTAN was a poet of the seventeenth century, and he used the tools of his trade and of his times to express himself. But beyond the *pointes,* the conceits, and the preciosity, lie a sensibility and a sensitivity so universal that they reduce all artifice to subservience. That is what makes Tristan appear ever fresh, even to modern readers and jaded critics of "things Baroque." Going well beyond his contemporaries in that realm, he gave us the most refined expression of the anguish that so characterized their protean world, and no less of what Amédée Carriat called "the dangerous seduction of illusion."[1] His anguish at the realization of the fragility of dreams—of the vanity of the effort to maintain an aura of enchantment at the very moment of its disintegration—is one most readily shared by any sensitive reader. All the thematic and metaphoric commonplaces of his day are to be found in his work, but with such a personal coloration and such deep conviction, that they are renewed, made palatable, and strike responsive chords in our innermost being. What at first reading may appear to be a mere exercise in rhetoric, frequently reveals itself under closer scrutiny as a sterling expression of profound sensibilities. Tristan, a court poet, had to play a certain game; but it was a game that demanded to be played seriously and consciously—one that was to be played with equal skill by artists such as Watteau, Verlaine, and Debussy.

There is, perhaps, no better example of this process of personal renewal than the poem "L'Ambition tancée" *(La Lyre).* The theme was already a hackneyed one when Marino treated it in his "Memento homo quia cinis" *(La Lira);* and Tristan's first quatrain is a very close adaptation of Marino's—though I personally believe that Tristan's treatment of the parallel images is a far more polished one:

120

Aux rayons du Soleil, le Paon audacieux,
Cet Avril animé, ce firmament volage,
Etalle avec orgueil en son riche plumage
Et les fleurs du Printemps, et les Astres des Cieux.[2]

The second quatrain of Tristan's sonnet continues in the Marinistic vein, but the tercets offer a radical break: as Tristan moves from the dazzling display of the quatrains to the meditation of the tercets, the harsh sonorities of the former yield to a deliberate pace and muted sonorities. The medium has become part and parcel of the message. Much the same can be said of "Stances à M. de Saintot" (*La Lyre*), a long poem somewhat spoiled by interminable examples and pedantic references. It is worthy of mention here because it too adds a beautiful personal timbre to commonplaces. Tristan begins hesitantingly, with chaotic rhythms, to list all the negative aspects of the human condition, only to end the poem on a positive note, the last stanzas literally soaring on wings of song. Tristan's fears are posited, but so are his convictions that man must have a concept of his dignity and of his worth. As in the beautiful "L'Orphée," Tristan begins with a baggage of clichés and manages to turn it into a poignant expression of personal feelings.

II *The Dramatist*

In *La Vida es sueño*, Calderon observes that man is "the monster of his labyrinth, one he builds himself and in which he loses himself." Created by man's own conscience, it will only release its victim if the latter is capable of virtuous will. Narbal, at the end of *La Mariane*, says no less to Hérode: "You are the artisan of your own misfortunes" (1806). Corneille's Auguste is "Master of the universe," because he is first "master of himself." The Hérodes and Osmans of Tristan are, first and foremost, victims of their own passions which isolate them. Their solitude and impotence is a poetic, as well as a dramatic, function of characters who never quite realize their essence—or who do not fully comprehend what that essence entails. They seek a dialogue which is made impossible by they themselves as much as by those who surround and—wittingly or unwittingly—torment them. When the sought-after dialogue becomes impossible, these victims of their own passions, lost in their labyrinth, lapse into a state of self-deception consecrated by madness and stilled only by death.

Tristan seems at his best when he describes rejected or spurned people expressing their sorrow or rage. It is easy to see in this phenomenon an autobiographical revelation. Such a tendency is also deceptive in its promise: up to a point, it is merely the belaboring of the obvious; past that point, it is gratuitous. A frustrated poet, in a world he no longer recognized as one guided by proper values, he was bound to lavish his greatest lyrical outpourings on characters with whose travails he could empathize, and in the description of whose passions he could blend convention and personal sensibility. In the most poignant scenes of his tragedies—and, not too strangely, in the most hilarious ones of his comedy—it is this aspect of his art that comes through more readily, and which, uniting poetry and drama, makes the best of these plays still viable today: probing investigations by a sensitive human being into the basic nature of the human condition.

III   *Matthew XIII, 57*

"A Prophet is not without honor save in his own country and in his own house."

In one of his moments of self-deprecation, Tristan wrote:

> Je ne fais point ces vers de choix
> Par qui l'oreille est enchantée:
> On enveloppe des anchois
> De Mariane et de Panthée. (*Amours*, "Lettre à DD")

But he knew his worth, and in the dedicatory letter of *La Mort de Sénèque*, he aired a sentiment that he was to echo over and over: "The Muses have no brush that I cannot handle with some dexterity." And, basically, his contemporaries agreed. His plays were performed frequently, with both financial and artistic success. His plays and his poems had numerous editions, both in France and abroad. And, for several decades, he was well represented in every worthwhile anthology. Not all of his work is of equal merit, and the kindest critic must sooner or later realize that Queen Christine of Sweden was right when she declared his work uneven.[3] Whatever the verdict of that distant queen may have been, Cyrano de Bergerac was undoubtedly closer to the general verdict of the time when he called Tristan "the only poet, the only philosopher, and the only free man that you have."[4]

With the advent of the "Classical" period, Tristan fell from favor. For two and a half centuries, in spite of the work of Bernardin, Tristan L'Hermite was, if not entirely forgotten, at least thoroughly neglected. During the first half of this century, thanks to editions of his works by Jacques Madeleine and his inclusion in anthologies compiled by such poets as Valery Larbaud and Max-Pol Fouchet, he managed to come out of that neglect. But it was not until after the Second World War that he really came into his own. Only with the renewal of interest in the Baroque were his works dusted off and his genuine merit recognized. Since that time, interest in his works, both dramatic and poetic, has not ceased to grow.

Ironically, though this Renaissance must be credited in large part to the efforts of Amédée Carriat, himself a prizewinning poet and a constant champion of Tristan, and though a few of Tristan's plays have been performed—rarely—in France, the impetus for the continued growth of interest in the man and his work comes from abroad. With the exception of J.-P. Chauveau's edition of *La Lyre*, the critical editions of Tristan's works have all been authored abroad— principally in Italy, Canada, and the United States. Brilliant articles on Tristan have been authored in France, where most school manuals echo Antoine Adam's sentiments, namely, that Tristan was the greatest poet of the age of Louis XIII; but almost all the full-length studies of his work come from Italian, British, Canadian, or American academic centers.[5]

In all these studies, in all these editions, it is apparent that "la plus noble figure de poète que puisse offrir le siècle de Louis XIII," to repeat Antoine Adam's verdict, is still able to strike responsive chords today with flashes of Modernism, which makes us think of Valéry, Apollinaire, Prévert, and even Jarry.[6] What is even more apparent, is that he speaks to us across the ages in a universal and eternal language of sensitivity; his lyricism, in spite of all its intellectualism and conventionality is imbued with an ever youthful and zestful spontaneity, even in his most pensive lines:

> Mon plus secret conseil et mon cher entretien,
> Pensers, chers confidents d'une amour si fidèle,
> Tenez-moi compagnie . . .[7] (*Amours*, "Agréable pensées")

Notes and References

Preface

1. (Limoges, 1955).
2. (Paris, 1946), p. 7.

Chapter One

1. Only one has ever been attempted, that by N.-M. Bernardin, *Un Précurseur de Racine, Tristan L'Hermite, Sieur du Solier (1601–1655)* (Paris, 1895). Though dated and with many errors, it is still very useful.
2. Also spelled Solier, Soulier, Souliers.
3. See *Le Page disgracié* (Paris, 1946), p. 55.
4. For a description of this milieu and its vagarious principals, see my *Gaston d'Orléans et sa cour: Etude littéraire* (Chapel Hill, 1963).
5. *La Lyre*, p. 68. "Let destiny run its course. . . . I will go home to forget the grief whose reason I cannot understand."
6. For some tentative ones, see my *Gaston*, pp. 74–76, and "Le Succés inexpliqué de *La Folie du sage*", *Romance Notes* 3 (1961), 25–29.
7. *Plaintes*, p. 103.
8. *La Lyre*, p. 68. "As one sees after the frost, with which winter freezes our land, the sweetness of spring reborn, so my days will come out of their night."
9. *Vers héroïques*, pp. 148–49. "I see that Gaston abandons me. . . . In this misfortune, I must guide my hope toward the most charming mistress that could ever boast of Heaven's favor."
10. A. C. Lefort de la Morinière, ed., *Bibliothèque poétique* (Paris, 1745), I, 290. "Acting like a dog lying at the lord's feet."
11. The religious poems were published posthumously, in 1665, in *Les Exercices spirituels,* only two copies of which are still known to exist. *La Coromène* has been lost.

Chapter Two

1. *Recueil de pièces en prose les plus agréables de ce temps* (Paris, 1658), pp. 324–31. Judging by the style, the "Carte du Royaume des précieuses" that precedes it may also be by him.
2. It is worth noting that Louis-Urbain de Caumartin, son of Louis-François, was a close friend of Voltaire.

3. It is interesting to note that the second edition of the *Principes* came out in 1643, thus coinciding with the centenary of Copernicus's refutation of the theocentric theory.

4. *Histoire de la littérature française* (Paris, 1962), II, 141.

5. *Literature as a System* (Princeton, 1971), pp. 74 ff.

6. The page is disgusted by the lechery of a young Englishwoman who, half intoxicated, tries to seduce him in the very bed shared by her dead-drunk husband, a seduction that ends in disaster when the "shameless beauty" vomits all over the page's head. But he laughs at jokes perpetrated on others, though these pranks frequently involve maiming or death. (See particularly Bk. II, Ch. 30–33, 38–39.) The influence of Spanish and Italian *conteurs* and novelists is undeniable; equally so is that of French novels such as the *Astrée*, of all the elements of salon literature that permeate his poetry, but the quasi précieux language, the refinement—relative to the genre (one has only to compare this tone with the far cruder one of the Realistic novels of Sorel and Scarron)—the grace and easy wit, the gentle, never virulent irony, the understated and reticent descriptions of the crudest biological functions, only heighten the everpresent physicality, as when he speaks of this "belle impudente" who becomes a victim of her intoxicated lubricity: "Il lui prit un certain mal de coeur qui déshonora toute ma tête." (Her nausea "dishonored" his head, as he barely had time to avert his face.)

7. As a page enjoying the proximity of the private life of the royal family, seeing and commenting on a side of courtly life seldom shown in any literature, he gives the modern reader a rare glimpse to be appreciated. As he follows the king in his military expeditions, relating the glory and the misery of such campaigns—there is a particularly vivid description of the epidemic that decimated one expedition against the meridional Protestants—his narrative makes evident that the times were, beneath the well known veneer of politeness and decorum, coarse, crass, and cruel. Even Tristan, known for his virtue and kindness, time and time again enjoys jokes that reveal the perpetrator to be—by today's standards, at any rate—quite devoid of sense and sensitivity.

8. For a thorough discussion of Tristan's letters in the context of the epistolary genre of that time, see Catherine Grisé's introduction to her edition of the *Lettres meslées* (Geneva, 1972).

9. *Op. cit.*, p. 562.

10. Catherine Grisé, in her introduction to the letters, has drawn numerous parallels between certain letters and poems on the same subject, amply demonstrating the omnipresence in Tristan's work of diverse themes and sentiments, particularly concerning freedom and servitude (political or erotic), fate and fortune, etc.

11. *Lettres* (Paris, 1647), p. 65.

12. *Lettres*, pp. XXIII-XXIV.

13. The Italian "heroic" letters, however, were written in verse.

14. *Lettres*, pp. XXVII-XXVIII.

15. *Ibid.*, p. 132.

Chapter Three

1. "Artifice and Sincerity in the Poetry of Tristan L'Hermite," *Modern Language Notes* 74 (May, 1959), 422–23.

2. Bernardin had suspected this, but could not prove it.

3. The best known example of this is Rostand's Roxane, who cannot love Christian unless his feelings are helped out of their "labyrinth" by Cyrano's brilliant wit.

4. *Tristan, ou l'Eloge d'un poète* (Limoges, 1955), p. 96.

5. "Artifice and Sincerity," p. 427.

6. *Vers héroïques* (Geneva, 1967), p. 155. "Cool, somber, and solitary night, holy repository of all great secrets, be they of war or of love, night, mother of rest and nurse of those wakes that produce such marvels, grant me advice worthy of the light of day."

7. *Vers héroïques*, "La Servitude." "Would I lower myself in thousands of ways, lay siege to twenty doors to tear away some bread not even proffered?"

8. *La Lyre*, "Daphnis, fais-moi raison." "Of what use is great renown after death?"

9. *Plaintes*, "A l'Honneur de Sylvie." "I do not regret having followed you and thank you for the sacred secrets you have taught me. . . . And sure henceforth of my poems' excellence, I can without insolence accept laurels on my hair . . . [because an immortal beauty assures my own immortality:] she finds extreme sweetness in my style and readily confesses that I have much grace in demonstrating her rigor."

10. "Narcisse baroque," *Nouvelle Revue Française* (1 Sept., 1961), p. 558.

11. *Lettres meslées*, Letter 81.

12. *Les Amours*, "Le Prélude." "I do not write of the burning of Troy . . . but only of the tears in which I drown. . . . So I do not expect that the reputation of my verse, carrying my own to the ends of the universe would give me immortality: I want to gain less honor than love; others wish to cause envy, I only aspire to gain pity."

13. *Vers héroïques*, "L'Extase d'un baiser." "This kiss is a seal that ends my life; and as one can find a serpent under flowers, so have I met my death on a rosebud."

14. "My blood is drying up, a burning fever robs me of color and reason; Heavens! I have gathered on that beautiful lip a celestial nectar and a deadly poison."

15. *Les Plaintes d'Acante*, "Les Cheveux blonds." "Fine gold of price beyond compare, clear sunrays, sweet and subtle texture [pun, since *trame* means "texture" or "trap"] whose soft expanse has waves of fire in which Love has drowned my reason a thousand times. Beautiful hair, your freedom is a betrayal: must you, by showing yourself, hide my lady from me? Was it not

enough to captivate my soul without imprisonning this beautiful body? But O gentle golden seas, your pride is being humbled; under the dexterity of the hand that contains you, you will, like I, lose your freedom. And I have the pleasure of seeing for once in my life, that by tying the beautiful hair that has arrested me, one has taken the freedom of that which took it from me."

16. *La Lyre.* "Beautiful anomaly of nature, it is true that your face is extremely black, yet perfectly beautiful, and the polished ebony which is your ornament bests the whitest ivory. O divine marvel unknown to our times, that a dark object shine so brightly, and that an extinguished coal should burn more acutely than those who still maintain a flame. Into these black hands I give my liberty; I who was invincible before all other beauties, am kindled by a Moor, tamed by a slave. But hide, o sun, you who come from the place whence came that star which, to your shame, bears night on her face and daylight in her eyes."

17. If in Marino's poetry, the metaphor is seldom more than an intellectual game or lexical gymnastics, in Tristan's, its purpose is always to communicate some message.

18. *Flowers of Evil*, "Correspondances."

Chapter Four

1. Liminary poem to *Lettres mêlées du sieur du Pelletier*, (Paris, 1642).

2. "Prosopopée de F.T.L." "Raised at court from earliest youth, I courted fortune but never obtained anything from her, for I loved Virtue, that proud mistress who makes one defy trouble and scorn wealth."

3. "Dazzled by mundane splendor, I always flattered myself with vain hope, acting like a dog lying at a great lord's feet. I was ever poor, yet tried to be seen, I lived in need waiting for fortune, and died on my trunk while awaiting my master."

4. "Tristan L'Hermite et la célébration des héros," *Baroque* 3 (1969), 117.

5. (Paris, 1654).

6. "Your soul aspires only to good; your heart abhors vice and your valor undertakes nothing without first consulting justice."

7. It is interesting to note that a recurring example of such degeneration is the bad ruler, a further example of Tristan's attachment to the feudal ethos.

8. N.p., n.d.

9. "Tristan L'Hermite et la célébration des héros," p. 121. Chauveau's expression—"à l'instant précis où son destin se joue"—is particularly fortunate, because it suggests the playing out of a role fixed by the fates, as a dramatic role might be fixed by an author.

10. "And barely can one find in the grass the foundations of its proud palaces."

11. The Milanese snake and the Sicilian Vespers are but two of the many

heraldic and historic allusions in Tristan's ode celebrating Gaston's Picardy expedition (*La Lyre*, "Pour Monseigneur le Duc d' Orléans").

12. Lines 241–50. "It is then that with lines born of high inspiration I will show the universe that your valor is superhuman. My writings will be so imbued with light, pomp, art, and beauty that Envy will become livid and, lowering its eyes in shame, will think that Apollo himself has recorded the deeds of Mars."

Chapter Five

1. "Flattered by the gentle noise of a brook, with a clearer and more beautiful spirit, as if to spite the painting that Nature spreads all about, I will undertake your portrait."

2. One of the best examples of this in painting is P. Patel's "Paysage composé avec ruines antiques," in the Louvre. The geometric severity of the ruins is constantly interrupted by wild natural features, light and darkness are decidedly fighting for supremacy, and details alternate with hazy, "Impressionistic" areas.

3. On the other hand, whenever a poet tries to describe such paintings, it ends up in failure: the painter can give a sense of what he feels, as can the poet. But when the latter tries to describe the work of the former, he must try to graphically enumerate what was intended as a very personal impression. The painter obviously chooses to select a few salient features, and to highlight them; the poet now adds his own selective process. How is he to create a tableau by describing a few of its features? How is the reader to reconstitute the entity from this catalog devoid of linearity, of focus, and of perspective? Tristan's "Maison d'Astrée" is an example of such an attempt at description which utterly fails to create (or recreate) a "picture."

4. Ironically, this artist is not above discussing the artificiality of the process with another artist, and in "L'Orphée," dedicated to a multifaceted artist, Tristan speaks of the "painted" feathers of birds, of the "ingenious" nightingale, "harmoniously" singing "Motets" with "artifice." The frequency of references to art reveals the pleasure of the artist acknowledging the game that all his peers must play. The skill of the creator is obviously not tested by avoiding clichés, but by renewing them.

5. The same phenomenon can be seen in "La Mer" and, for dew, in "Promesse à Philis."

6. "The waves, enameled in green, which seem like carved jaspers, steal his face from each other and, by little shivers, show thousands of diamond spurs instead of his image. . . . Coursing diligently, the waves, in long folds of glass and silver, come to break on the shore, where their remains on each occasion cause a living source of pearls to spurt among the rocks." These "pearls" seem far more appropriate when appearing as dew on the petals in "Promesse à Philis."

7. Poussin's "Winter" is subtitled "The Flood," and its religious message is obvious.

8. "The flowers at this first awakening seem to open in joy and to turn to the sun to adore Your wisdom. The little birds in the woods honor with diverse voices the Author of this new-born light."

9. Only recently, in "A Reading of Tristan L'Hermite's 'La Mer,' " *Papers on French Seventeenth-Century Literature* 9 (1978), 11–28, has R. T. Corum destroyed that myth.

10. "Narcisse baroque," *Nouvelle Revue Française* (September, 1961), 558.

11. *Ibid.*, p. 561.

12. "The sun is setting; the splendor with which it bursts paints over there in the West a great scarlet river."

Chapter Six

1. "Gentle and peaceful night, comforting deity whose realm is so favorable to those who are tired from the long toil of day, everyone sleeps now under your humid veils, but in spite of your poppies, the thorns of love force me to stay awake with the stars."

2. "I do not know what invincible star, to which all is possible, has poured me this secret poison . . . and forbids my senses to listen to reason."

3. "I see her ravishing waist, I notice her bursting throat on which floats her beautiful hair, these precious nets and these fatal plaits which create new labyrinths for liberties and which tie hearts with indissoluble knots."

4. This metaphor is repeated in the dedication of *La Mort de Chrispe* to Mme. de Chaulnes, in which Tristan describes her as the star presiding over the play's birth, hopefully to assure its good fortune.

5. "Fate, whose rigor, contrary to beautiful things so soon tarnishes roses, has the greatest anger for the most beautiful things" (with a pun on "objet," the *précieux* term for beloved).

6. "Fate, tyrant of things beautiful, allows the bright blaze of roses to last but a moment."

7. "Unrelenting time, which goes light-footedly, takes with it all beautiful things: it is to warn us to husband it well and gather bouquets during the season of roses."

8. "In the misfortunes which one cannot avoid, to torment oneself is to increase one's woes; one must yield to this highest law without murmuring, and by the strength of a constant heart, when one cannot avoid ill fortune, one affronts it by bearing it." Cf., Horace, *Odes*, ending of I, 24.

9. I do not wish to imply that Tristan is a faithful disciple of Epicurus, for Tristan's belief in the omnipotence of the stars prevents him from accepting the Epicurean idea of free will. Without going into the details that exploring such a question demands—the entire century centers many of its theological struggles around this momentous question—one has but to remember that

Tristan considered most of the circumstances and events of his life as the direct result of the stars' positions—from the description of the astrological conditions that prevailed at the time of his birth (*Le Page disgracié*, ch. 2), to the apologies for all that has happened to him, "the toy of the passions of stars and fortune" (*Ibid.*, ch. 1); see also *La Lyre*, "Le Navire." In this respect at least, Tristan was neither Epicurean nor Christian.

10. "By a fatal and harsh law from which no mortal is exempt, our great Isabelle is in her tomb, and the heavens have opened to be enriched by the rarest treasure that ever was."

11. See Doris Guillumette, *La Libre pensée dans l'oeuvre de Tristan L'Hermite* (Paris, 1972).

12. *Eloge*, pp. 72–76.

13. "The Religious Poetry of Tristan L'Hermite," *Mosaic* IV–4 (1971), 16. This independence would partially explain his insecurity at the court of Gaston.

14. *L'Autre monde* (Paris, 1968), p. 77.

15. Only in his ballets does Tristan demonstrate daring iconoclasm and obscenity, but his libretti are on a par with all the others of the time, even those of ballets danced by Louis XIII and Richelieu.

16. *Eloge*, pp. 72–76.

17. *La Muse historique* (Paris, 1877), II, 96.

18. Catherine Grisé, "Religious poetry," p. 15. For further information on this phenomenon, see Terence Cave, *Devotional Poetry in France* (Cambridge, 1969), particularly the opening chapters.

19. "Let your Spirit enter my heart; let its divine ardor melt the ice of such a great obduracy; and though my sins demand justice, do not allow me to perish in this blindness."

20. *Introduction à la vie dévote*, pt. 1, ch. 11.

21. "I followed the flock of sinners; drinking in the same cup, I became intoxicated by the wine of sensuality; and the habit taken in that extreme confusion has reduced me to the point where iniquity itself is the punishment for my iniquities."

22. "During this holy fast under which our bodies wail for forty days, sweet savior, whose mercy is never exhausted, hear our humble pleas, be our succor."

23. "Out of the red waters, victors over the tempest, decked in clothes radiantly white . . ."

24. Since much of the devotional poetry had been launched by Humanists, the mixture was to be expected. Referring to one of his own metaphoric sonnets, La Ceppède likened Orpheus's descent into hell to save his Eurydice to that of Christ for the sake of mankind (*Théorèmes* (1617; rpt. Geneva, 1966), I, 385).

25. *Introduction à la vie dévote*, pt. 2, ch. 13. See also St. Augustine, *Epistles* CXXX, 10 for a similar exhortation. The exercises to which I refer here, however, are more sustained in tone and more specific in intent.

26. "For the sake of my soul, forget your capture; break the chains to free it and deliver who captured you."

27. In many of these representations of the passion (as in some of the prayers to the Virgin), the Mary-Christ relationship is used to postulate the physical-spiritual dichotomy and the times' attempt to reach spiritual understanding by means of representations of the material world. In "Prière à la Sainte Vierge," the metaphors are almost all centered on this mixture of abstract and concrete, the body being "the living tomb of the soul."

28. Cave, p. 47.

29. "Religious Poetry," p. 23.

30. "Out of the depths of sorrows that fill my soul, and from the midst of the evils that I feel besetting me, my voice rises unto you, my God, I beg you to give ear to it."

31. "I deserved death and you pardoned me, I was worthy of hatred and you loved me."

32. "Lord, I call out, engulfed in crime, to your great kindness toward these great depths which are always vaster than our iniquity. Though my sins deserve punishment, instead of punishing me according to your justice, please forgive me according to your mercy."

33. "I recognize my error; a dull sadness stings and gnaws at me ceaselessly and a secret tormentor fills me with fear; my heart is ever struck by it. The horror of my misdeeds fills me with fear and my sin forever rises against me."

34. "Turn your eyes from my transgressions; make as to forget my disobedience whose ungratefulness moves you to anger. Fill my soul with a new grace and in my breast create a new heart, but one which loves you and is yours forever."

Chapter Seven

1. *Jean Racine* (Boston, 1977), pp. 27–28.

2. Ernest Serret, "Un Précurseur de Racine, Tristan L'Hermite," *Le Correspondant* (25 April, 1870), pp. 334–54; N.-M. Bernardin, *Un Précurseur de Racine: Tristan L'Hermite* (Paris, 1895).

3. *La Crise de la conscience européenne* (Paris, 1935).

4. Much of what follows is heavily based on my *The Strangers: The Tragic World of Tristan L'Hermite* (Gainesville, 1966).

5. Meursault is executed not for the murder of an Arab, but because he did not cry at his mother's funeral.

6. Sénèque and Fauste kill themselves, but not by choice. Their "suicides" are merely the implementations of imperial edicts.

7. All references following citations from the plays are to line numbers as assigned in the critical edition of the *Théâtre complet* (University, Alabama, 1975).

8. On the physical level, he is the torturer, she the victim. On all higher levels, of course, the roles are reversed.

9. Lacy Lockert, *Studies in French Classical Tragedy* (Nashville, 1958), pp. 119, 132.

10. Maurice Baudin, *The Profession of King in Seventeenth-Century French Drama* (Baltimore, 1941), p. 39.

11. If Montdory's brilliant career had to be curtailed by an apoplectic stroke, how sublimely ironic that it was to be during a performance of this play.

12. He has four lines in Act IV and twenty-four in Act V. We do not know enough of the chronology of the play's composition, but it is logical to surmise that the role, initially conceived for Montdory, was reduced when that actor suffered his stroke. I am conjecturing that Tristan, ill and demoralized—see his prefatory letter—did not revise what he had already written, but reduced Araspe's role in subsequent acts.

13. "Govern his mind as well as his subjects, and tempering justice with extreme mercy, in commanding others, command himself." As can be seen, justice, for a monarch ruling by divine right, allows anything, but magnanimity must be present as a tempering virtue.

14. At the end of the text, after the traditional "Fin," Tristan added the motto "Nil solidum," a reflection not only of the dramatic *dénouement*, but also of his own sentiments concerning himself.

15. "O gods! if you knew what it is like to love."

16. "I thought I saw his shape and his eyes and his complexion; the real sound of his voice struck my ear, his face was merry, his mouth red, he was thanking the gods for the joy of seeing me again, and his happiness could be read in his eyes."

17. "Your altered face has not changed my soul; you are but ice and I all in flames: my heart is opened by the blows that wounded you; although you are gone, I have not left you; my spirit still follows your shadow as it flies away, and my dying mouth is glued to yours."

18. In the tragic world of Tristan, lucidity normally reigns supreme; *Panthée* is, obviously, the exception.

19. "Here is my offering, O liberating God. God of whom the recent news has delighted my soul, God who is only love, spirit, light and life, God of the man of Tarsus [Saint Paul], in whom I place my hope, my soul comes from you, please welcome it."

20. His long duet with Constance is more concerned with political realities and hopes for the future than with love, and always remains properly dull.

21. "Fauste, how will you decide between love and virtue which today keep your soul in suspense? Already fear and desire set up alliances in your mind. You must let go or grasp, it is time to choose."

22. Daniela Dalla Valle, *Il Teatro di Tristan L'Hermite* (Torino, 1964), p. 263.

23. He will, however, acknowledge that he is touched by her great love a few moments later (1387–90). The passionate declaration of the girl momentarily weakens his resolve—for he finally sees in her a kindred spirit—but it does not destroy his *vertu*.

Chapter Eight

1. "Old wrinkle-faced monkey derided by all the pages and whose name is enough to make crying children quiet, old image of death who so bothers us with the sorrow of your old age, to tell the truth, time is too lazy in dragging you to the tomb."

2. "Here lies a drinker whose soul was delighted whenever he filled it with old or new wine; I think that he would not regret life if there were some broached casks in his tomb."

3. Puns on horns—symbols of cuckoldry—are used repeatedly by Tristan in his burlesque poems, even those included in serious collections, as in "Prosopopée d'un Hercule de bronze" of the *Vers héroïques*.

4. "This pedantic parasite with a wild expression wants the table to be set as soon as he enters, and everything that he swallows is digested more quickly than if he had one hundred mad wolves in his stomach. Hunger forever mutters in his bowels; you could not find a more gluttonous monster if you sought him from pole to pole; in short, he is so carried away by his gluttony that he once bit a passerby on the shoulder because he smelled like a shoulder of lamb."

5. *Vers du ballet de Monseigneur Frère du Roi* (Paris, 1627). "Beauties who, to keep the linings of your cabinets cleaner, sweep both on holidays and Sundays, come to me: I promise you a broom handle that will never break." These words were accompanied with appropriate gestures by an "emmancheur de balais" (a broom handle fitter), while his friends multiplied the allusions to the horns they intended to set on all husbands' foreheads. In all fairness to Tristan and Gaston, it must be added that such ballets were the norm, and even those danced by Louis XIII and Richelieu were no less obscene.

6. For instance, compare the first scene of *La Folie* to the scene between Claudius and Polonius in *Hamlet*, or the expression of the King's gratitude to the scene between Claudius and Laertes.

7. See Michel Foucault, *Folie et déraison: histoire de la folie à l'âge classique* (Paris, 1961).

8. See H. Hauvette, *La "Morte vivante"* (Paris, 1933).

9. The ensuing attack on doctors, the physical healers who have failed him no less than the philosophers, is a natural progression.

10. "Am I not King?—Yes, Sire, but I am a father.—But a subject.—But of a heart both too noble and too frank to prostitute to you his blood so unworthily. . . .—You speak somewhat proudly.—But with justice.—Your

life is at stake.—Then I will die. But at least I will give up the ghost with my honor."

11. In Rotrou's play, some robbers interfere; their intervention is totally unprepared. The satyrs, on the other hand, are both delightful and logical participants: early in the play, they witness the girls in unguarded moments of play and banter, and gleefully discuss their lascivious plans to abduct them. When they later try to bring their plans to fruition, they offer a golden opportunity for one of the lovers to display his courage and devotion.

12. Jacques Madeleine, in his critical edition of *Le Parasite* (Paris, 1934), p. XXII, suggested that this was due to Tristan's illness. Perhaps. It could just as readily have been due to his lack of interest.

13. See Corneille's "Examen" of his *Galerie du palais*.

14. "Old ruffle-feathered crow, plastered statue, moving antique, defleshed skeleton, ambulatory tomb, conspiratorial tax-gauger, king of thieves the corner of whose eyes look like spurs, and whose temples are as hollow as sauce-boats . . ."

15. "Damned be love and whoever meddles in it; let the Devil take the knave whose best valets have an empty stomach while delivering love notes." (There is an effective and appropriate pun on *poulet*, which means both "chicken" and "love letter.")

Chapter Nine

1. *Eloge*, p. 7.
2. "At the rising of the sun, the audacious peacock, that animated April, that flying firmament, spreads with pride in its rich plumage, both the flowers of Spring and the stars of Heaven." Marino's version reads as follows:

> Ecco il pomposo augel, ch'al nuovo giorno
> Spiega il gemmato suo vario monile,
> Quasi di fior, quasi di stelle adorno
> Picciolo Cielo, e animato Aprile.

(See the pompous bird, which at the break of day displays the gems of its variegated necklace, adorning, as with flowers, as with stars, the little sky, this animated April.")

3. That, at least, was the report of Urbain Chevreau to whom Tristan had entrusted some *stances* for the Queen, in the hope that she would become his patron.

4. *Etats et empires de la lune* (Paris, 1921), I, 36.

5. Most of these are, unfortunately, unpublished dissertations. For the monolingual reader, it is even more unfortunate that of those published, only my *Strangers* is in English.

6. Carriat, *Choix de pages* (Limoges, 1960), p. 16.

7. "My most secret counsel and my dear sustenance, thoughts, dear confidants of so faithful a love, keep me company . . ."

Selected Bibliography

PRIMARY SOURCES

1. Early Editions of the principal works:

Les Plaintes d'Achante. Paris: La Fosse & Dauplet, 1633; Anvers: Aertssens, 1633. Tristan's first *"recueil."*

Les Amours de Tristan. Paris: Billaine & Courbé, 1638. Reproduces much of the *Plaintes* greatly augmented by new poems.

La Lyre. Paris: Courbé, 1641.

L'Office de la Sainte Vierge. [Paris: Des Hayes, 1646.] No complete copy of this edition known in any public library.

Les Heures dédiées à la Sainte Vierge. Paris: Loyson, 1653. New title for unsold copies of *Office*.

Les Vers héroïques. Paris: Loyson & Portier, 1648.

Les Exercices spirituels. Paris: Loyson, 1665.

La Mariane. Paris: Courbé, 1637.

Panthée. Paris: Courbé, 1639.

La Folie du sage. Paris: Toussaint Quinet, 1645.

La Mort de Sénèque. Paris: Toussaint Quinet, 1645.

La Mort de Chrispe. Paris: Cardin Besongne, 1645.

La Célimène de Mr de Rotrou. Accommodée au théâtre sous le nom d'Amarillis, Pastorale. Paris: Sommaville & Courbé, 1653.

Le Parasite. Paris: Courbé, 1654.

Osman. Paris: Luynes, 1656.

Lettres mêlées. Paris: Courbé, 1642.

Le Page disgracié. Paris: T. Quinet, 1643.

2. Modern, critical editions:

Les Plaintes d'Acante et autres oeuvres. J. Madeleine, ed. Paris: Cornély, 1909. Not "critical" in the modern sense, but the best edition available.

Une réparation posthume due au "Précurseur de Racine". François L'Hermite, Sieur du Solier, poète chrétien et catholique. F. Lachèvre, ed. Paris: Clavreuil, 1941. Partial, uncritical edition of the *Heures*, but most readily available.

Les Vers héroïques. C. M. Grisé, ed. Geneva: Droz, 1967. Splendid critical edition.

La Lyre. J.-P. Chauveau, ed. Geneva: Droz, 1977. Superlative critical edition.

Théâtre complet. C. Abraham, J. Schweitzer, J. Van Baelen, eds. University: University of Alabama Press, 1975. Though there are editions of separate plays, this is the only one of the complete theater.

Lettres meslées. C. Grisé, ed. Geneva: Droz, 1972. Fine critical edition, with truly enlightening introduction.

Le Page disgracié. M. Arland, ed. Paris: Stock, 1946. Not really critical, but with a sensitive introduction and relatively safe text.

SECONDARY SOURCES

1. Bibliographies:

CIORANESCU, ALEXANDRE. *Bibliographie de la littérature française du dix-septième siècle.* 3 vols. Paris: CNRS, 1965–66. The most complete of the available bibliographies, very useful in spite of some errors and omissions.

CABEEN, DAVID C., and JULES BRODY. *A Critical Bibliography of French Literature, Volume III: The Seventeenth Century.* Syracuse: Syracuse University Press, 1961. This volume, edited by Nathan Edelman, while far from complete, should be the most useful to the general reader insofar as it judiciously comments on the items selected for inclusion. Sadly out of date, it must be used with its forthcoming supplement or with Gravit, et al.

GRAVIT, FRANCIS W., et al. *Bibliography of French Seventeenth-Century Studies.* Bloomington: Indiana University, 1953–68; Washington: George Washington University, 1969–71; and Fort Collins: Colorado State University, 1972 to date. Although there have been changes in the editorship of this annual bibliography, published for the Modern Language Association French Group III, it is still called the "Gravit Bibligraphy." While not truly critical, it is carefully annotated and, for the general reader, the most useful existing supplement to the "Cabeen."

KLAPP, OTTO. *Bibliographie d'histoire littéraire française.* Frankfurt: Klostermann, 1956 to date. Appearing every two years, this is the most complete of the periodic bibliographies.

2. Dictionaries:

DUBOIS, JEAN, RENE LAGANE and ALAIN LEROND. *Dictionnaire du français classique.* Paris: Larousse, 1971. Indispensable for the understanding of archaisms.

GRENTE, CARDINAL GEORGES. *Dictionnaire des lettres françaises. Le dix-septième siècle.* Paris: Fayard, 1954. First rate for biographical sketches with longer articles for selected topics.

3. Literary, Historical, Social, and Political Background:
(In view of the wide selection available, only books in English are suggested here.)

BENICHOU, PAUL. *Man and Ethics; Studies in French Classicism.* Garden City: Doubleday, 1971. Translation by E. Hughes of a brilliant work.

BRERETON, GEOFFREY. *French Tragic Drama in the Sixteenth and Seventeenth Centuries.* London: Methuen, 1974. Thorough, eminently readable synthesis.

CRUICKSHANK, JOHN. *French Literature and its Background. II: 17th Century.* Oxford: Oxford University Press, 1968. Work of a large team of scholars; the value of its intelligent insights is enhanced by chronological charts, synoptic tables, and a comprehensive index.

HOWARD, W. D. *The Seventeenth Century.* London: Nelson, 1965. Very learned, yet eminently readable book on life and letters.

LOUGH, JOHN. *An Introduction to Seventeenth-Century France.* New York: McKay, 1969. Unpretentious. As good an introduction as one could wish for.

YARROW, P. J. *A Literary History of France. Vol. II: The Seventeenth Century.* New York: Barnes and Noble, 1967. Though without the broad base of Cruickshank, this is a fine book, perhaps the best of its kind in English, with a superlative section on theater.

4. Tristan Criticism:

(Relatively little has been done in English on Tristan; the following bibliography is perforce polyglot. For a list of the numerous articles devoted to specific aspects of Tristan, see the Carriat bibliography, below.)

ABRAHAM, CLAUDE. *The Strangers. The Tragic World of Tristan L'Hermite.* Gainesville: University of Florida Press, 1966.

BERNARDIN, N.-M. *Un Précurseur de Racine. Tristan L'Hermite.* Paris: Picard, 1895. In spite of its age, still the standard literary biography of the man.

CARRIAT, AMEDEE. *Tristan ou l'Eloge d'un poète.* Limoges: Rougerie, 1955. Sensitive appreciation by the foremost Tristan scholar of today, himself a prize winning poet.

————. *Bibliographie des oeuvres de Tristan L'Hermite.* Limoges: Rougerie, 1955. Critical bibliography, completed and brought up to date in "Tristan L'Hermite," in *Dictionaire bio-bibliographique des auteurs creusois.* Guéret: Lecante, 1972.

————. ed. *Cahiers Tristan L'Hermite.* Mortemart: Rougerie, 1979–. A new journal devoted exclusively to Tristan. In addition to articles, a thorough bibliography that corrects and completes previous ones.

DALLA VALLE, DANIELA. *Il Teatro di Tristan L'Hermite.* Torino: Giappichelli, 1964. By far the best work on Tristan's drama.

GUILLUMETTE, DORIS. *La Libre pensée dans l'oeuvre de Tristan L'Hermite.* Paris: Nizet, 1972. Diligent attempt to settle a thorny issue. Extremely useful index.

Index